SOLOMON ISLANDERS IN WORLD WAR II

AN INDIGENOUS PERSPECTIVE

SOLOMON ISLANDERS IN WORLD WAR II

AN INDIGENOUS PERSPECTIVE

ANNA ANNIE KWAI

STATE, SOCIETY AND GOVERNANCE IN MELANESIA SERIES

Published by ANU Press
The Australian National University
Acton ACT 2601, Australia
Email: anupress@anu.edu.au
This title is also available online at press.anu.edu.au

 A catalogue record for this book is available from the National Library of Australia

ISBN(s): 9781760461652 (print)
          9781760461669 (eBook)

All rights reserved. No part of this publication may be reproduced, stored in a retrieval system or transmitted in any form or by any means, electronic, mechanical, photocopying or otherwise, without the prior permission of the publisher.

Cover design and layout by ANU Press. Cover photograph: 'Members of Donald Kennedy's coastwatching group in training at Seghe Point, New Georgia, June 1943', by Michael Currin, courtesy University of Hawai'i Hamilton Library collection.

This edition © 2017 ANU Press

Contents

List of Figures vii
Acknowledgements ix
Preface xi
1. Introduction 1
2. Islanders at War 15
3. Why Support the Allies? 51
4. Impacts of the War 75
5. Monument-building and Nation-building 93
6. Conclusion 113
Appendix 1: Prime Minister Derek Sikua's letter of endorsement
of the Solomon Scouts and Coastwatchers Trust 119
Appendix 2: Letter of recognition from President Barack Obama . . . 121
Bibliography 125

List of Figures

Figure 1: Unveiling of the Pride of Our Nation monument, 7 August 2011 2

Figure 2: Map of Solomon Islands 4

Figure 3: Locations of coastwatcher stations, Solomon Islands 17

Figure 4: Sergeant Harry Wickham, British Solomon Islands Defence Force and Major M.S. Currin (with two scouts) meet on a trail in the Munda area of New Georgia. 19

Figure 5: The coconut husk used by J.F. Kennedy during the war. . . . 28

Figure 6: Members of Donald Kennedy's coastwatching group ('Kennedy's Army') in training at Seghe Point, New Georgia, June 1943. Billy Gina stands over the man sighting his rifle. . . . 30

Figure 7: Daniel Kalea 32

Figure 8: Members of Donald Kennedy's coastwatching group ('Kennedy's Army'), wearing mostly captured Japanese helmets, in formation at Seghe Point, New Georgia, June 1943 34

Figure 9: Martin Clemens and his scouts (standing left to right: Daniel Pule, Martin Clemens, Andrew Langabaea; seated left to right: Olorere, Gumu, Chaparuka, Chaku) 37

Figure 10: Scouts of the western Solomons in a *tomoko* canoe 41

Figure 11: AWA Teleradio 3BZ used by coastwatchers during the war. 42

Figure 12: Scout Salea (centre) and ammunition carriers (right) with Colonel Hill's troops at Aola, Guadalcanal, 10 October 1942 44

Figure 13: Lieutenant Colonel Carlson's supply train, Guadalcanal . . 45

Figure 14: Makira women and children watch as men from their island leave for labour corps work with the Allies on Guadalcanal, June 1943 48

Figure 15: Workers line up to receive weekly wages of five shillings (80 cents) from Australian Major J.V. Mather, Guadalcanal, 28 January 1943. Note the military cameraman at work 69

Figure 16: Nggela people go out to trade with sailors on board the USS *Nicholas* anchored in Purvis Bay, 22 August 1943..... 84

Figure 17: Lieutenant George Rollinsk, supply officer of 193 Infantry dickers, with three natives selling canes and grass skirts, New Georgia, 2 December 1943 85

Figure 18: Artist Frank Haikiu's design of the Pride of Our Nation sculpture, 2009 94

Figure 19: The Pride of Our Nation monument.................. 95

Figure 20: Japanese War Memorial............................ 97

Figure 21: Guadalcanal American Memorial, 2017............... 98

Figure 22: Sir Jacob Vouza monument, 2013 101

Figure 23: Frank Haikiu (second from left) with Solomon Scouts and Coastwatchers Trust Medal recipient Sebastian Ilala and members of the Australian military during the 2015 ceremony at Commonwealth Street, Honiara...................... 104

Figure 24: Rt Hon. Baroness Ann Taylor lays a wreath at the Pride of Our Nation monument 106

Figure 25: The Duke and Duchess of Cambridge at the reopening of Commonwealth Street, 2012........................ 110

Acknowledgements

The completion of this book would not have been possible without the support of so many people. First, I would like to express my sincere gratitude to Dr Frank Bongiorno, for his assistance, guidance and feedback throughout the planning and development of my Master of Arts thesis, which was the genesis of this book. I also thank Dr Andrew Connelly for his moral support, patience and encouragement throughout the writing process. *Tagio tumas* Professor David Akin for the detailed feedback on my thesis draft, which helped shape the book into what it is now. To Professor Geoffrey White, many thanks and appreciation for directing me to relevant scholarly materials and for your academic support throughout the process; your feedback was significant to this publication. To Dr Chris Ballard, I couldn't thank you enough for all your support; thank you so much for your mentorship, friendship and wisdom. To Rear Admiral James Goldrick and Moana Tregaskis, I am forever grateful the time you gave my first draft and providing useful feedback. Enormous thanks to Chris Chavelier and Dr Rebecca Monson for being such wonderful friends. Your advice, encouragement and endless academic and moral support during my time at The Australian National University helped me survive; I couldn't achieve success without friends like you. I'm also thankful to Dr Vicki Luker, for your friendship, interest in my work and support; thank you so much for encouraging me to publish my work.

Thanks to Tony and Marie-Claire Saunders, my dear friends and extended family. *Tagio tumas* for all the friendship and wonderful company at Port Germein. Marie-Claire, thanks for reading my drafts and providing useful feedback.

My very special thanks to Sir Bruce and Lady Keithie Saunders, for taking me under your wing as your daughter. Your constructive ideas, enthusiastic encouragement, passion, friendship, leadership and continuous moral support have inspired me to pursue further studies. I'm blessed to have you as family.

To the patron of the Solomon Scouts and Coastwatchers Trust Board, Hon. Milner Tozaka, thanks for your leadership, humility and friendship. My sincere appreciation to the members of the trust board both past and present: it has been a pleasure working with you. To the remarkable ambassadors of the trust, John Innes and Dr Martin Hadlow, *tagio tumas wantoks* for the intelligent discussions, sharing your knowledge and your friendship. You're true ambassadors.

I was fortunate to have met the late Oneisimo Tadangoana, late Alfred Alasasa Bisili, late Edward Lulumani and late Beato. This book is dedicated to you. Thank you very much for inspiring me to write about your stories.

Stefan Armbruster, *tagio tumas* for being the voice of the trust. Your work is a blessing to our efforts. Thank you so much for all the publicity through Special Broadcasting Service (SBS) Australia. To Peter Flahavin, I hope to meet you someday and thank you very much for sending me your archival pictures of Solomon Islands.

To Dr Greg Terrill (your wonderful family and mother Pam), thank you so much for believing in me. Your humility, friendship and mentorship mean a lot. *Tagio tumas*!

Thank you as well to Andrew Byrnes, for showing great respect and interest in my work and, in your capacity as the Australian High Commissioner to Solomon Islands, for your support of the trust. To the Australian Government, many thanks for the scholarship, which helped me pursue further studies and led to the publication of this book.

To my friends, Angelina Fakaia, Joy Basi, Florence Gibbs, Patricia Pollard, Anke Mösinger, my super sisters Wendy Anikwai and Jerolyn Taro and my wonderful brothers Watson Anikwai, Michael Anikwai and Chris Ofotalau, *tagio tumas* from the depth of my heart. Your friendship inspires me to keep pushing on.

And to my family at home — in Honiara, on Malaita and Makira — an enormous thank you. My parents, aunts and uncles: I will never thank you enough no matter how hard I try. Words can never express my gratitude to you. God has blessed me with your unconditional love and support. For that, I am forever grateful.

Finally, to all my friends, colleagues and those who contributed to my work in one way or another whom I forgot to name here (please forgive me), thank you so much for your support.

Preface

World War II is a significant period in the colonial history of Solomon Islands. As I will discuss throughout this book, it shaped the political and physical foundation of the country. The histories of battles fought in the Solomons theatre of war are among some of the well-documented histories in the world. However, most of these histories consist of dominant narratives of non-indigenous origin. Within these outsider narratives, Solomon Islanders, although clearly exercising choice and agency while playing an active part in the campaign, are often simply regarded as loyal and pliant subjects of the British protectorate administration. This perception, among other factors, pushes aside any islander-centred analysis of the war in Solomon Islands.

My interest in the history of Solomon Islanders' involvement in the war stems from my childhood curiosity at seeing unexploded ordnance and other war relics along the Guadalcanal coastal plains. My father worked for the former Solomon Islands Plantation Limited, and I grew up on one of the company stations. Every weekend, my parents would take us fishing at the beach and on the way we would stop at a coconut plantation and collect dry coconuts. Piled under one of the coconut trees were old artillery shells about 30 centimetres long. The first time my little brother and I found the explosives there were 12 in total, but every time we stopped for coconuts we would count the bombs and each time the number decreased. People (mostly young men) would take one and place it in dry brush and set it on fire, out of curiosity and as a form of entertainment.

During my primary and high school years, we studied the histories of major wars and political events in other parts of the world, ranging from World War I and World War II, the Suez crisis and the Middle East crisis of 1973, to the Vietnam War, Korean War and the Cuban missile crisis. No history lesson involved the study of Solomon Islands history in World War II. When I started university, the only knowledge

I had of World War II in the Solomons were the bombs and other relics I saw during my childhood. Added to this lack of knowledge was my embarrassment ensuing from a conversation with an American exchange student I met at the University of the South Pacific in Suva who impressed me with her knowledge of the Solomons Campaign, information I was ignorant about. This drove me to learn more about the war. In the process of job hunting after university, I met Sir Bruce Saunders at a Rotary club meeting in Honiara. Sir Bruce spoke about his passion for doing something about the history of the coastwatchers and the importance of their work during the war. I'd never heard of the coastwatchers, but I listened with great interest and expressed my wish to become part of the effort. A few weeks later, I started working with Sir Bruce and others to develop the Solomon Scouts and Coastwatchers Trust. Part of my job was to educate myself on the history of the scouts and coastwatchers. It is from this engagement that I came to realise both the significance of local efforts during the war and the absence of local narratives in published histories. I feel it is my responsibility to tell these stories as a Solomon Islander would. I am not able to include all the heroic local stories, but I hope this book will inspire other Solomon Islanders to document more historical narratives coming down from older generations.

1
Introduction

On 7 August 2011, the mid-morning sun rising over the city of Honiara promised another hot but fine day. This was no ordinary day in the capital of Solomon Islands.[1] Over Commonwealth Street, in the heart of the city, loomed a strange, 4-metre-tall object covered by a silky grey fabric, with blooming tropical flowers around its base, which seemed to have appeared overnight. On one side of the object was a podium and two large white tents with chairs arranged facing the entrance to the street, a short but wide and busy thoroughfare leading from the main road through the city, past office buildings to the bustling wharf area. At the entrance, a pair of policemen in blue uniforms directed traffic and motioned invited dignitaries towards the tents; the curious people of Honiara, young and old, assembled along the street wondering what could be hidden under the grey shroud.

Echoing in the near distance as the last guests took their seats, a police siren announced the arrival of the governor general. The master of ceremonies spoke into a microphone, 'Please rise for the arrival of the governor', and everyone stood up as a police band played the national anthem. Despite the mid-morning tropical heat, the crowd beyond the VIP tents stood quietly in the sun as the official ceremony commenced. After a series of speeches and wreath laying, the speaker again summoned everyone to rise as the governor general, Frank Kabui, stood up to remove the grey fabric,

---

1   Contrary to popular usage, the official name of the country is 'Solomon Islands', not 'The Solomon Islands'.

and the long-awaited object was unveiled (Figure 1). The curiosity of the crowd spilled over as locals, expatriates and journalists all surged forward to get a glimpse.[2]

Figure 1: Unveiling of the Pride of Our Nation monument, 7 August 2011
Source: Photo by Anna Kwai.

2   Anna Kwai, personal observation, 7 August 2011.

1. INTRODUCTION

It was a new monument, built to recognise local contributions to the Allied Solomon Islands Campaign during World War II. Designed and sculpted by local artist Frank Haikiu, the monument consists of a concrete sculpture of three Solomon Islander scouts surrounding a European coastwatcher facing seaward on a 2-metre-high plinth. On the seaward side of the plinth, the famous words of wartime United States Navy Admiral William 'Bull' Halsey are inscribed: 'The Coastwatchers saved Guadalcanal and Guadalcanal saved the Pacific'. On the opposite side are the lesser known words of the Australian coastwatcher John Keenan: 'If it wasn't for local help I don't know what we could've done, we wouldn't have lasted 10 minutes'.

This book will examine the involvement of indigenous islanders in the Solomon Islands Campaign of World War II. It will show that the dominant narratives of the participation of islanders in the war are often rendered as simplistic representations of local wartime 'loyalty' to the Allied forces, and especially to the Solomon Islands' British colonial masters. But subjecting the efforts of islanders to a more detailed analysis reveals a more complex scenario — one that takes into account the varied nature of colonial influence on indigenous subjects and the effects the war had on postwar and contemporary Solomon Islands society. Understanding the complexities of islander wartime participation is important for balancing received representations of the indigenous war experience. As accounts of the war begin to find their way into the nation's school curriculums, more indigenous perspectives are needed to enable a comprehensive understanding of the war and its impacts on the development of the nation.

Historical background

The Solomons group comprises over 900 islands, scattered over an area of approximately 28,000 square kilometres in the South Pacific, east of Papua New Guinea and north-east of Australia, roughly aligned into two parallel island chains running north-west to south-east (Figure 2). The country has a population of around 500,000 people: a predominantly Melanesian population occupies the larger islands, while the smaller islands of Rennell and Bellona in the south and Ontong Java and Sikaiana in the north-east are inhabited by Polynesians (Pacific Islands Forum Secretariat n.d.). More than 80 different languages are spoken by the peoples of the Solomons, making it one of the Pacific's most diverse countries in terms of language and ethnicity.

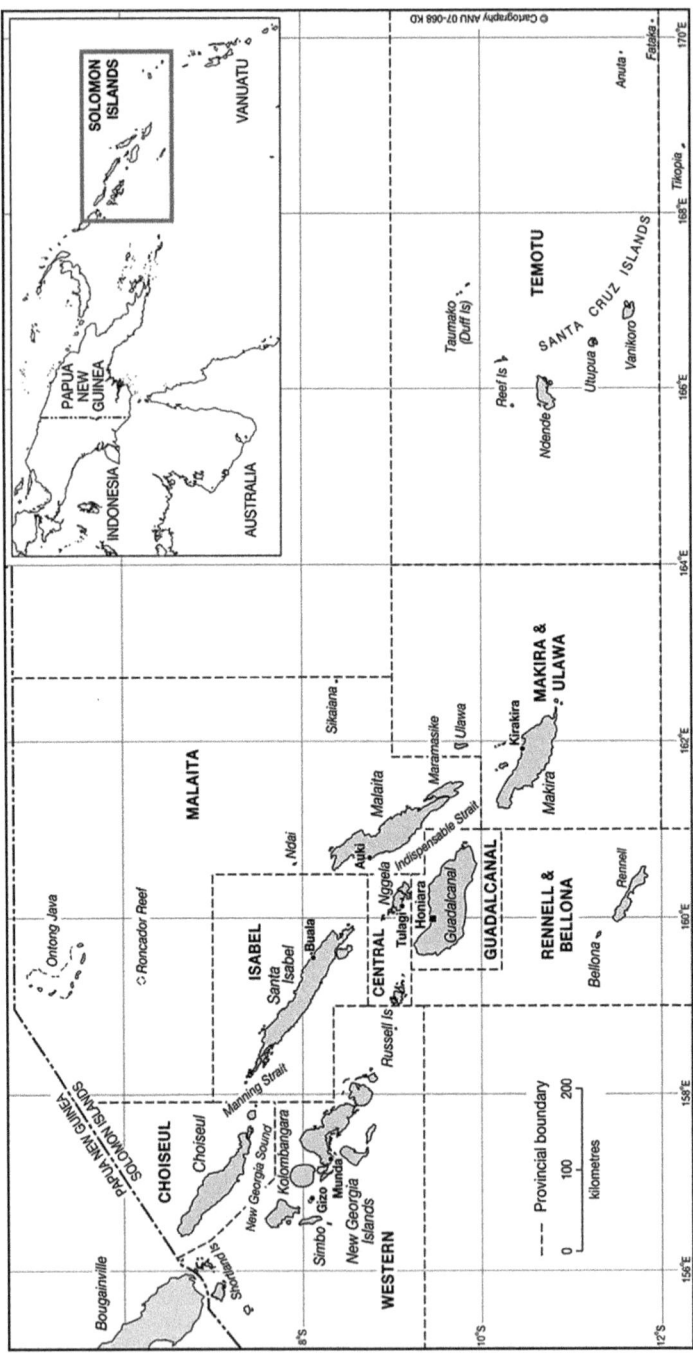

Figure 2: Map of Solomon Islands
Source: CartoGIS, College of Asia and the Pacific, The Australian National University.

1. INTRODUCTION

Indigenous peoples settled the large islands of the Solomons archipelago well before European exploration. Settlement on these remote islands occurred in the form of migration believed to be from Southeast Asia about 30,000 years ago (Matisoo-Smith et al. 1998). By the time the first European explorer, Álvaro de Mendaña y Neira, reached the Solomons in 1568, the large islands of the archipelago were well colonised by indigenous peoples. When Mendaña and his crew landed on the island he named Guadalcanal, he found alluvial gold. This led him to believe the island must have been where the biblical King Solomon's fabled mines were located; hence he named the group *Islas Salomon*, or 'Islands of Solomon'. Following a gap of around 200 years, a number of explorers, traders, whalers and missionaries visited the Solomons group. By the early 1800s, the local inhabitants were accustomed to the arrival of foreigners on their shores (Green 1976). By 1874, due to the growing need for labourers to work on large plantations in Queensland, Fiji and Samoa, islanders were forcibly recruited on a large scale in what became known as 'blackbirding'. This illegal recruitment continued to escalate throughout the Solomons and neighbouring islands, such as Papua New Guinea and Vanuatu. The British declared a protectorate over the Solomons in 1893 to put an end to this illegal labour trade (Belshaw 1950). An administrative centre was established at Tulagi on Gela Island in the Nggela (Florida) Islands four years later, and the English naturalist and Pacific adventurer Charles Morris Woodford became the first resident commissioner of the British Solomon Islands Protectorate. Under the influence of the colonial administration, the indigenous inhabitants of the islands were exposed to Western education, Christianity, new technologies and a filtered glimpse of the world beyond their shores. The common practice of tribal warfare was suppressed throughout the islands; by the early 1940s, such tribal conflict was rare. For nearly half a century, the Solomon Island group was a fairly neglected outpost of the colonial empire, but things were about to change.

On 7 December 1941, the Japanese Empire made its historic attack on the American fleet on Pearl Harbor, and on other American, British and Dutch possessions throughout Southeast Asia and the Pacific. These attacks shook the protectorate as much as they did the United States and its Allies. On 22 January 1942, the British Solomon Islands Protectorate experienced the shock of modern war as a Japanese plane dropped the first bomb on Gavutu in the Nggela (Florida) Islands. Japanese forces occupied Rabaul in the neighbouring Australian territory of New Guinea the following day.

Japanese troops pressed forward into the protectorate on 3 May 1942, but they arrived in Tulagi to find a ghost town; the colonial administration had relocated to Auki on Malaita, and nearly all European civilians had been evacuated to Australia. Most Europeans who chose to remain were enlisted with the Royal Australian Navy's coastwatching network and went into hiding in the jungles of Guadalcanal and other islands. Assisted by islanders, they spied and reported on Japanese activities.

The Japanese were unopposed in the British Solomon Islands Protectorate for over three months, during which time they constructed an airfield on Guadalcanal (COI 1946: 17). The news of the airfield was not welcomed by United States military intelligence. Its completion would threaten United States supply and communication lines to its Allies in the Pacific, especially Australia. On 7 August 1942, 11,000 men of the United States First Marine Division landed on Guadalcanal and Tulagi; their objective was to capture the airfield. This landing marked the beginning of the Solomon Islands Campaign: a campaign that lasted for over a year and resulted in the deaths of 23,800 Japanese and 1,600 United States soldiers (Miller 1995: 350).[3] In his 1995 book, *Pacific Turning Point*, historian Charles Koburger argues that the Solomons Campaign was, in fact, the turning point in the Pacific War and not the Battle of Midway as stated in most general histories of the Pacific War (Koburger 1995: 119). For Solomon Islanders, the campaign marked a new era in their history and continues to influence social, political and economic landscapes in the country today.

More than 50 years after World War II, the country underwent another major disruption: an outbreak of open conflict between the people of Guadalcanal and Malaita. Among other factors that triggered 'the tensions' were issues of ethnicity and postwar economic centralisation on Guadalcanal as a result of the war. Although the arrival of the Regional Assistance Mission to Solomon Islands (RAMSI) eventually ended the turmoil, the nation suffered drastically in terms of loss of national identity and pride.[4] In 2009, as part of a national restoration process, the Solomon

---

3   These figures do not include those on both sides who lost their lives at sea.
4   RAMSI was a joint effort by Pacific island countries led by Australian and New Zealand military and police forces. It was the result of Australia's response to the Solomon Islands Government's call for help to end hostilities between members of the Malaita Eagle Force and the Isitabu Freedom Movement on Guadalcanal. RAMSI initiated its program in Solomon Islands in 2003, four years after the crisis began. RAMSI's efforts resulted in the successful restoration of peace throughout the country. In June 2013, RAMSI celebrated its 10th anniversary in Solomon Islands and announced its transition out of the country.

Scouts and Coastwatchers Trust Board was founded.[5] The project involved the construction of a memorial honouring islander efforts in World War II, with the intent of promoting national identity and pride, but also serving as an educational tool to transmit knowledge of islander participation in the war to younger generations of Solomon Islanders. Coordinated by its founder, Bruce Saunders, an expatriate Australian businessman, the project resulted in the erection of the sculpture memorialising the scouts and coastwatchers described above, an honour roll and a plaque to the Royal Australian Navy. Taken together, these individual installations carry the title of the 'Pride of Our Nation' monument.[6]

In Australia, similar sentiments promoting a national identity and historical consciousness have become the subject of commemorative initiatives such as 'Australia Remembers 1945–1995', which involved the construction of monuments and nationwide commemorative events. Marking the 50th anniversary of the end of World War II, Australia Remembers hoped to achieve a 'uniquely Australian' understanding of the war and bolster national identity (Con Sciacca quoted in Liz Reed 1999: 159). Motivated partly by Australian efforts towards nation building through war commemoration, and seeing the need for rebuilding national identity in the aftermath of the upheavals in Solomon Islands, Saunders expressed in a press conference how he hoped the Pride of Our Nation monument would become the 'Solomon Islands version of the Anzac legend and Remembrance Day in Australia and New Zealand'.[7] Although the Pride of Our Nation monument has impressed both the national and international communities, only time will tell how well it will achieve the objective of promoting national pride and identity among the people of Solomon Islands.

---

5   When the Board of Trustees was founded, it was given the name 'Guadalcanal War Memorial Project' under the Solomon Islands Government Charitable Act. In 2014, after much consideration, the board agreed to change the name of the organisation to 'Solomon Scouts and Coastwatchers Trust' to be more reflective of the history the organisation is promoting, which is a unifying Solomon Islands history of the war.
6   Although these individual installations were built and dedicated separately, they are now regarded as one monument.
7   Bruce Saunders, Solomon Scouts and Coastwatchers Trust press conference, 5 March 2010, Honiara. An audio of the press conference is in the author's possession. It is also available at the Solomon Islands Broadcasting Corporation library, Honiara.

Previous writings on the Solomon Islands Campaign

The history of World War II in Solomon Islands has been studied and documented in many aspects.[8] The participation of islanders was administered by coastwatchers who were enlisted by the Royal Australian Navy's coastwatching network, and the islanders' stories were often mentioned in passing when the exploits of coastwatchers were recounted in published histories. One account that provides a detailed narration of the work of coastwatchers comes from the commander of the coastwatching network, Lieutenant Eric Feldt. In his book *The Coastwatchers* (1991), Feldt reveals how the coastwatchers operated from their outposts in enemy-occupied territory. As commander of the network, Feldt knew the significance of the work his men did behind enemy lines and argued that 'without them [the coastwatchers] the course of the war in the Pacific would have been drastically changed' (Feldt 1991: 1). Yet, to a coastwatcher who did the actual job of 'hide and seek' behind enemy lines, their fate depended on their knowledge of the tropical island environment and their relationship with the indigenous population. In his book *Fire over the Islands* (1970), Dick Horton provides a concise description of his coastwatching activities but also describes and acknowledges the efforts of his indigenous companions. In the final chapter, Horton interprets islanders' attitudes towards the Japanese and credits their efforts, stating 'without the Islanders neither the Coastwatchers nor the armed forces would have been able to achieve so much or so easily … their contribution to the defeat of the Japanese invaders cannot be measured in material terms alone' (Horton 1970: 247). This sentiment appears repeatedly in several memoirs, diaries and histories published by coastwatchers after the

---

8   One of the earliest and most prominent records of the war was Richard Tregaskis's *Guadalcanal Diary*. Published in 1943 while the war was still raging, Tregaskis's diary provides an insight into the United States Marines' journey to the Solomons. A journalist by profession, Tregaskis began his war diary on 26 July 1942 on board a transport ship making its way to Guadalcanal. His diary gives an account of the beginning of combat and the privations endured by Allied troops on Guadalcanal until 26 September 1942, when Tregaskis left the British Solomon Islands Protectorate. A similar personal narrative is Robert Leckie's *Helmet for My Pillow*, first published in 1957. Like Tregaskis, Leckie provides an insight into the epic struggles faced by the United States Marines in the protectorate. These two accounts each resulted in the production of films: *Guadalcanal Diary* (1943 — one of the first feature films made about the Pacific War) and *The Thin Red Line* (1998), as well as the HBO miniseries *The Pacific* (2010). Beyond these, the battle for the Solomons has attracted historians and other writers who have extensively documented individual battles fought in the islands. Some of the general war histories (to name only a few) include those by Brian Altobello (2000), Charles Koburger (1995), Herbert Laing Merillat (2010) and John Prados (2013).

war. In his published diary, *Alone on Guadalcanal* (1998), district officer Martin Clemens presents his experiences as a coastwatcher on Guadalcanal during the Japanese occupation. His memoir gives us a glimpse of the life of a district officer and coastwatcher, but also allows us to see just how completely his fate was in the hands of his indigenous comrades.

Like those of Feldt, Horton and Clemens, Walter Lord's book *Lonely Vigil* (1977) also narrates the story of coastwatchers and their role during the campaign. Although Lord was not a participant, his work provides much detail of the operations of coastwatchers behind enemy lines. Despite focusing on the fate of coastwatchers, Lord also acknowledges islanders' part in the network. A series of coastwatchers' reports from the northern Solomons were compiled in A.B. Feuer's 1992 edited book, *Coastwatching in WWII: Operations against the Japanese on the Solomon Islands, 1941–43*, providing an insight into coastwatching operations on Buka and Bougainville islands in the Australian-mandated Territory of New Guinea. Although these islands are geographically part of the Solomons group, their inhabitants were administered by Australia. For the purpose of this book, I focus on indigenous inhabitants of the British Solomon Islands Protectorate.

A more general account of the campaign is Stanley Jersey's *Hell's Islands: The Untold Story of Guadalcanal* (2008). Jersey's work provides a balanced analysis of both American and Japanese developments in the protectorate. Chronological in its structure, *Hell's Islands* begins with the story of the few Australians of the Royal Australian Air Force in the protectorate and moves through to the evacuation of Europeans from the protectorate, the United States Marine Corps' landing on Guadalcanal and subsequent events of the campaign. Like other accounts from a military perspective, Jersey's work mentions islanders only in passing and as secondary to coastwatching efforts. Similar accounts that pay attention to islanders, if only in passing, include James Michener's *Return to Paradise* (1951). In a chapter of 14 pages titled 'Guadalcanal', Michener briefly described the British Solomon Islands Protectorate, but focused more on the island of Guadalcanal and the difficulties of the environment as experienced by Allied troops. Michener, however, compared the indigenous peoples of Papua New Guinea to islanders of the British Solomon Islands Protectorate and stated that the 'fidelity of Solomon Islanders is unbelievable' (Michener 1951: 185). Such comments have contributed to a somewhat simplistic image of the responses of islanders to the challenges of the war.

The story of the coastwatchers is indeed one of courage, never ceasing to attract an audience despite the passing of time. Patrick Lindsay retold the story of the coastwatchers in his popular history *The Coast Watchers: The Men Behind Enemy Lines Who Saved the Pacific* (2010). Lindsay's work emphasises the importance of the contributions of these few men to the Allied war effort in the Solomons and to ultimate victory in the Pacific.[9] Mike Butcher presents a comprehensive biography of Donald Kennedy and provides an in-depth view into Kennedy's personal life and relationships with indigenous people during his time as district officer in the British Solomon Islands Protectorate and elsewhere in the Pacific (Butcher 2012).[10] In his 2013 book, *Watriama and Co: Further Pacific Islands Portraits*, Hugh Laracy discusses the life and journey of Donald Kennedy in various colonies of the Pacific including the British Solomon Islands. He details Kennedy's style of leadership as protectorate district officer and coastwatcher prior to and during the war, and argues that in spite of Kennedy's flaws, he was extraordinarily talented and his contributions to colonial administration have gone largely unnoticed. Laracy's chapter serves as testimony to Kennedy's intelligence and 'remarkable talents' as a colonial officer (Laracy 2013: 211–28). In a chapter that follows, Laracy discusses the fate of native medical practitioner George Bogese, who was regarded as a 'traitor' to the coastwatching network and the Allied efforts in Solomon Islands. Laracy's analysis is important because it gives an understanding of the complex relationship between educated islanders and members of the colonial administration (ibid.: 229–42). In another chapter, Laracy discusses the work of another colonial officer, Hector MacQuarrie, who published *Vouza and the Solomon Islands* (1945). Laracy stated: 'despite the title … the book has little to say about the Solomons. Rather it is an episodic memoir about MacQuarrie's brief sojourn in a remote part of the group as a colonial administration officer' (Laracy 2013: 243–56). Although MacQuarrie's work does not contribute directly to our knowledge of war, his account of Vouza is important in understanding the nature of relationships between islanders and colonial administrators.

---

9   Peter McQuarrie (1994) wrote of the Micronesian coastwatching network.
10 Donald Kennedy was a New Zealander. He served as district officer in the British Solomon Islands Protectorate prior to World War II, and during the war became a key player in coastwatching efforts in the Solomons. A further discussion of Kennedy takes place in Chapter 3 in this book.

While these accounts narrate the story of the coastwatchers or their personal lives in detail, they do not provide adequate insight into islander participation, nor do they set out any extensive analysis of local experiences during the war. This is the gap I hope to help fill. While these earlier narratives relay the coastwatchers' story from a European, or 'outside', perspective, this book will examine the narratives of islanders who played a part in the war.

Starting in the late 1980s, a series of publications began to fill this gap in the literature through oral histories of local wartime experiences. The Western Province Assembly recorded and transcribed 32 oral stories of wartime participants with the aim of preserving recollections of those who served in Western Province (WPA 1988). A similar initiative resulted in the compilation of a special issue of *O'O: A Journal of Solomon Islands Studies* (Laracy and White 1988). This was the result of a week-long conference in Honiara in mid-1987 aimed at assessing regional experiences of World War II and their social, cultural and historical importance. In 1988, the Solomon Islands College of Higher Education and the University of the South Pacific published *The Big Death: Solomon Islanders Remember World War II* (White et al. 1988). This book was a transcription of wartime memories of local experiences and provided a space in which oral recollections of local veterans could be understood by the current generations of Solomon Islanders. These publications have been successful in their attempts to record and preserve personal and local stories. My aim in this book is to contribute further to these local histories and present my own perspective, as a Solomon Islander woman, examining local involvement in World War II. My perspective in this book stems from my encounter with the few local surviving veterans while working as a researcher and executive officer for the Solomon Scouts and Coastwatchers Trust. The recollections of some of these veterans were transcribed in earlier works mentioned above. However, none of these earlier materials provides a thorough evaluation of the nature of islander contributions to the war effort.

Local experiences in and contributions to the Solomons Campaign have been narrated mainly by outsiders, and local efforts have continued to be represented in simplistic terms of 'loyalty' (White 1995). As local oral recollections have begun to be documented and published, they have confirmed that the lives of the European coastwatchers often rested in the hands of the so-called uncivilised natives whom they governed. There indeed existed a great sense of loyalty towards the coastwatchers and those

Allied soldiers whose lives were saved by islanders. While inscribing this essential loyalty onto war monuments becomes relevant to modern-day nation-building, it is also important that the complexities of islander attitudes towards the war and the forces arrayed on both sides be better understood. This is to provide for a more comprehensive and nuanced understanding of islander involvement, and the changes that the war wrought on local perspectives, the social environment of those it affected and the perceptions of the world beyond the islands.

The resources consulted for this book are predominantly from Allied perspectives and islanders' oral recollections. Due to barriers of language, access and time, Japanese sources are not consulted and their perceptions of islanders during the occupation of the British Solomon Islands Protectorate are not discussed. Other resources that may be relevant to the topic of this book that are held in archives, libraries and museums outside Canberra and Solomon Islands have not been consulted. Moreover, when looking at the war from a Solomon Islander perspective, the literature available on the topic bears an almost entirely male perspective. While mentioning local women in passing, the discussions in this book inevitably reflect the lack of accounts of indigenous women's perspectives and their experiences during the war.

In the next chapter, I discuss the contributions of islanders to the Allied war effort on Guadalcanal. I argue that the nature and significance of islanders' roles in the Allied campaign tend to become blurred when narrated from an outside perspective. Solomon Islanders' involvement in the war was a significant contribution to the defence of the islands. Despite the presence of the Japanese military throughout the islands, the indigenous population remained predominantly supportive of the Allies until the end of the war.

Chapter 3 explores the complex factors that motivated islander participation and their sense of loyalty to the Allies. I argue that local involvement in the war was influenced by indigenous culture, the colonial government and observations of military developments in local contexts. This results in a depiction of local perspectives that reaches beyond the simple notion of loyalty that has been portrayed in outside narratives of the war. Understanding these complexities will help us comprehend how the war influenced the attitudes of islanders.

In Chapter 4, I discuss the extensive impacts of the war on island societies, politics and economy. I show that some of these impacts were experienced as immediate benefits for the development of the British protectorate, yet proved to be problematic in the long term.

My study concludes by discussing the recognition of local wartime contributions through the erection of the Pride of Our Nation monument dedicated on 7 August 2011, the anniversary of the Allied landing on Guadalcanal. I argue that the monument is more politically relevant than its historical legacy first indicates. While sociopolitical problems faced in contemporary Solomon Islands are not entirely consequences of the war, I suggest that issues of ethnic disparity among the indigenous population were exacerbated by lopsided postwar reconstruction on Guadalcanal by the colonial administration. Realising these ethnic differences and addressing them in a collective manner through the construction of monuments in modern-day Solomon Islands can help to reimagine a wartime past that provides a common thread sewing together the history of an ethnically diverse nation. Hence, a closer understanding of the nature of local efforts will enable a more thorough sense of appreciation of islanders' actions during the war.

2
Islanders at War

After Rabaul was occupied by Japanese troops on 23 January 1942, the islands of the British Solomon Islands Protectorate to the south-east were the next target for conquest by the mighty Japanese Empire. The tide of Japan's expansion in the Pacific reached Faisi and the Shortland Islands in the northern Solomons on 31 March 1942. By early May, Japanese forces had occupied Tulagi, the official seat of the protectorate, and the neighbouring islets of Gavutu and Tanambogo. In July, Japanese troops landed on Guadalcanal and began the construction of an airfield. The establishment of a Japanese airfield on Guadalcanal was a disturbing development for Allied intelligence; it would threaten American supply routes to Australia and New Zealand, and pose a direct security threat to the United States Pacific Fleet's seaboard communication lines to India and the Persian Gulf (Feldt 1991: xvii–xviii). To counter these threats, the United States First Marine Division under the command of Major General Alexander Vandegrift landed on Guadalcanal and Tulagi on 7 August 1942. The Japanese airfield, which was near completion, was captured on the following day and named Henderson Field after a United States flyer killed at the Battle of Midway (Lord 1977: 37–8). This amphibious landing marked the beginning of the 'Battle of the Solomons' or the 'Solomons Campaign', which lasted more than six months and included a long series of hard-fought land, air and sea battles. This chapter aims to show how islanders were absorbed in the Allied effort of the campaign and to put into perspective the part they played as well as the significance of their contributions to the eventual Allied victory.

The coastwatching network

In order to understand the efforts of islanders in the Solomon Islands Campaign, it is necessary to put the Royal Australian Navy's coastwatching network into context. Almost immediately after World War I, Captain C.J. Clare, a district naval officer in Western Australia, proposed a national security initiative: a secret intelligence network that would engage civilians residing in coastal areas of Australia to gather intelligence on any subversive or suspicious developments and activities in their surroundings. Captain Clare's suggestion resulted in a staff paper that was submitted to the chief of staff at the navy headquarters in Melbourne. The paper strategically suggested that the proposed security scheme should not be limited to Australia but should also be extended to include the Australian colonial territories of Papua and New Guinea, and the British-administered Solomon Islands. It was observed that these islands north and north-east of Australia would be vulnerable if foreign powers were to launch an attack on Australia, and would likely be the first crown soil in harm's way. Lieutenant Commander Eric Feldt, the head of this network at the outbreak of World War II in the Pacific, saw this area north-east of Australia as a 'fence' with many gates to guard (Lord 1977: 7). Feldt was aware of the gaps in surveillance along this vast fence and first envisioned them filled by coastwatchers, choosing the code name 'Ferdinand' for the proposed network of personnel. Ferdinand the Bull was the title character in a popular children's book by Munro Leaf, initially published in 1936. Feldt recalled:

> I chose Ferdinand ... who did not fight but sat under a tree and just smelled the flowers. It was meant as a reminder to Coastwatchers that it was not their duty to fight and so draw attention to themselves, but to sit circumspectly and unobtrusively, gathering information. Of course, like their titular prototype, they could fight if they were stung (Feldt 1991: 95).

By December 1941, when the United States of America declared war on Japan, the coastwatching network was already well established and encompassed much of the south-west Pacific. Over 100 coastwatchers were stationed in a 2,500-mile arc from the western end of the Territory of New Guinea, through Papua and the Solomons, to the New Hebrides. Most of these coastwatchers soon found themselves behind enemy lines. Equipped with very heavy wireless radios and supported by local scouts, they moved from place to place seeking vantage points and radioing information back to Resident Commissioner William Marchant on Malaita, where it was further communicated to Port Vila and from there on to the South Pacific Area and South West Pacific Area commands.

There were 23 coastwatching stations in the Solomons group, extending from Bougainville in the north-west to San Cristobal in the south-east (Figure 3). Of all the coastwatchers, only Hugh Wheatley, Harry Wickham and Geoffrey Kuper were Solomon Islanders, and they were of mixed-race origin. The rest were European: district officers of the British Solomon Islands Protectorate, plantation owners and managers and missionaries. But whether black or white, they all had in common considerable knowledge of local culture, traditions, environment and people — the knowledge that was essential for intelligence operations behind enemy lines.

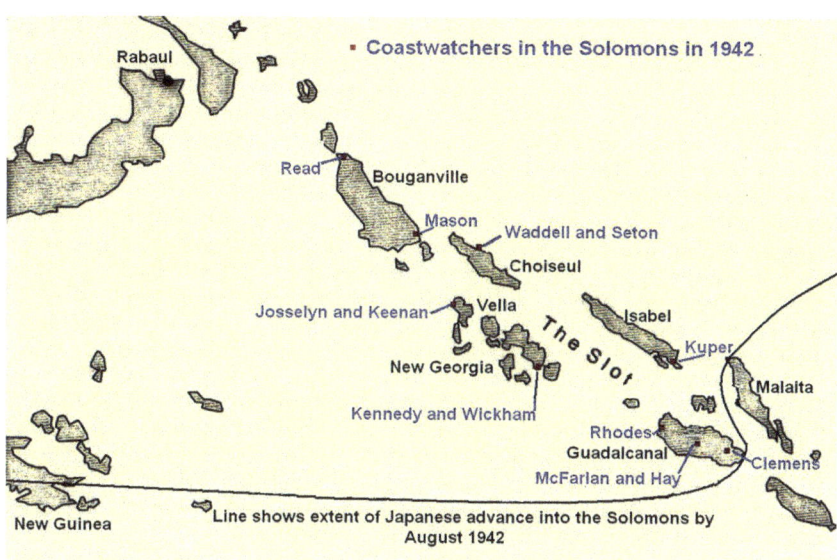

Figure 3: Locations of coastwatcher stations, Solomon Islands
Source: Courtesy of John Innes.

In this section, I will focus on the coastwatchers of islander origin, for it was mainly under the coastwatching scheme that islanders served during the campaign. Hugh Wheatley was a native medical practitioner (a British colonial government position) by profession. He was appointed as coastwatcher by Donald Kennedy, district officer for Isabel and the Central Islands. This was a rather informal appointment that was not approved by the resident commissioner. Perhaps Kennedy saw the need for a quick expansion of the coastwatching network and so made appointments without consulting his superiors. In early March 1942, Wheatley received reports regarding an outbreak of Spanish influenza in the Shortland Islands. He decided that he should travel to the Shortlands to assess the situation and to treat victims of the disease. He left for the Shortlands with a radio given to him by Kennedy, who had tasked him with extending the coastwatching network while performing his medical duties. Wheatley arrived on the island a day before Japanese troops landed at Faisi. Almost immediately, and before he could participate in the coastwatching network, he was taken prisoner by the Japanese on 6 April 1942. He was later sent to Rabaul as a prisoner of war (Clemens 1998: 42). In September 1942, Wheatley and others were transferred to a Japanese military prison in Rabaul where he continued to provide medical assistance to wounded and sick prisoners of war in the prison facility until his death in May 1944.

More successful in coastwatching than Wheatley was Harry Wickham (Figure 4), a trader and plantation manager residing in Roviana Lagoon. Also appointed a coastwatcher by Kennedy, Wickham became a real asset to the network, engaging in organising islanders for scouting and reconnaissance, participating in the rescue of fallen pilots and seamen, reporting enemy movements and developments and assisting in the evacuation of rescued Allied personnel. Wickham's coastwatching station at New Georgia became a safe haven for pilots and sailors whose planes had been shot down or vessels sunk by Japanese forces in the vicinity. Although Wickham was active as a coastwatcher until the fighting ended in the Solomons, little of his story is featured in written records. Walter Lord mentions him only in passing, when Wickham met coastwatcher Dick Horton in New Georgia on 23 December 1942. Horton, whose mission was to observe enemy activities on Munda, was relieved to meet up with Wickham. Lord wrote that Wickham 'knew every foot of the area … if anybody could find the right spot for watching the Japanese at Munda, he would be the one' (Lord 1977: 123).

2. ISLANDERS AT WAR

Figure 4: Sergeant Harry Wickham, British Solomon Islands Defence Force and Major M.S. Currin (with two scouts) meet on a trail in the Munda area of New Georgia
Source: Photo by Michael Currin, courtesy University of Hawai'i Hamilton Library collection.

Perhaps most remarkable for his efforts as coastwatcher was native medical practitioner Geoffrey Kuper. Like Wheatley and Wickham, Kuper was of mixed race with a Caucasian father and local mother. He was appointed as a coastwatcher by Martin Clemens, district officer on Guadalcanal, and assigned under Kennedy to run the coastwatching station on Isabel Island. Kuper's role as a coastwatcher was to plan and execute operations with his team of scouts, with the goal of obtaining intelligence information on Japanese movements. Like other coastwatchers, he also organised search and rescue missions, carried out guerrilla attacks against Japanese forces and ensured the safe return of rescued airmen and sailors to Allied bases.

Kuper, who became a regular voice in Allied radio traffic, also liaised with coastwatchers on Bougainville Island to confirm Japanese planes and ships heading towards Guadalcanal to bombard Henderson Field and the Allied headquarters at Lunga. In Bougainville, for example, coastwatcher Paul Mason sighted Japanese planes and transmitted messages to Henderson Field such as 'forty bombers heading yours' (Lord 1977: 62). As soon as the planes were sighted by Kuper and other coastwatchers in the Solomons group, they would also radio Henderson Field to confirm sightings of the reported bombers. Their reports of approaching fighters and destroyers allowed Allied defenders to prepare for attacks. This early warning ensured sufficient time for the Allied bombers to depart the airfield and, more significantly, for Allied fighter planes to gain sufficient height to swoop down on the enemy and launch a surprise counterattack with devastating effects, inflicting catastrophic losses on the Japanese. It also assisted Allied bombers in attacking Japanese convoys supplying their troops on Guadalcanal. The importance of coastwatchers' contributions to Allied efforts in the British Solomon Islands Protectorate and territories of Papua and New Guinea during the war with Japan is memorialised at the coastwatchers' lighthouse honour plaque in Madang Province, Papua New Guinea, which bears the inscription: 'They waited and warned and died that we might live'.

The fact that these three locals were of mixed race enabled them to be appointed coastwatchers, a position of authority over 'pure-blooded' islanders in the racialised colonial hierarchy of indigenous administration during the escalation of Japanese military developments in the British Solomon Islands Protectorate. Mixed-raced islanders were regarded as inferior to Europeans but above 'pure' islanders. Lord wrote about Geoffrey Kuper that 'given the colonial world of the time, with its rigid racial barriers, there was no place for him in the white planter society of his father' (Lord 1977: 155). On the other hand, Joyce Wheatley Kevisi recalled that in the western Solomons Harry Wickham brought discomfort to villagers: 'people were afraid to see him come ashore. They knew that if the Japanese saw him [Harry] with them, they would be in trouble. So they didn't really welcome Harry' (WPA 1988: 67–70). These statements showed the betwixt and between position of mixed-race islanders in the British protectorate. Beyond Wheatley, Wickham and Kuper, the highest rank any islander achieved within the colonial interwar administration was second-in-command to a coastwatcher. Locals who obtained this rank included Andrew Langabaea, Bill Bennett, George Maelalo and the celebrated local hero Sergeant Major Jacob Vouza, whose stories will be discussed later in the chapter.

The scouting network

Integral to the coastwatching network were the Solomon Island scouts. Scouts were recruited by district officers and enlisted into the British Solomon Islands Defence Force. The scouting network can be divided into two categories: armed and unarmed scouts. The armed scouts were made up of police constables who had served in the British Solomon Islands Police Force prior to the war. Although not all of them were armed in the early stages of the campaign due to a shortage of rifles, most of them had received some training in handling firearms. According to Martin Clemens, by mid-1942 he had recruited 18 policemen armed with 12 serviceable rifles and only 300 rounds of ammunition. His entire garrison of scouts in Aola comprised 60 able men (Clemens 1998: 44). The unarmed category included scouts who were recruited during the course of war, when the need for swift intelligence reporting increased (ibid.: 17).[1] Enlisting as part of the British Solomon Islands Defence Force enabled scouts to gain a military rank. While armed and unarmed scouts followed different histories, for the purposes of this chapter both will be referred to as 'scouts'.

As the Japanese advanced into the Solomons, the need to recruit islanders to help coastwatchers in their fight against the invaders became pressing. More Solomon Islanders were recruited to serve in the scouting network. Islanders were engaged in three significant tasks under the network: gathering intelligence, conducting search and rescue missions and guerrilla warfare.[2]

Intelligence gathering

Local scouts were given the perilous task of gathering intelligence on Japanese operations in the islands. Some of the most hazardous operations were conducted during the early phases of the campaign, when the Japanese began construction of the airfield on Guadalcanal. Scouts were sent by their coastwatch commanders to seek employment at the Japanese

---

1   By later stages of the campaign, almost all unarmed scouts had been armed with weapons captured from Japanese forces. Clemens (1998: 17) stated that his scouts later collected six extra rifles, 2,500 rounds of ammunition and 'a number of useful weapons were ... captured'.
2   Despite the instructions of 'Ferdinand' to only observe and report information, coastwatchers and their scouts often engaged in guerrilla warfare against Japanese troops when they felt the need to protect themselves and their hideouts.

camp at Lunga, and then act as spies for the Allied forces by pretending to be curious civilians. Lieutenant D.S. Macfarlane of the Royal Australian Navy, who was in charge of the coastwatching station at Barande on Guadalcanal, sent his local 'cook boy' to Lunga to obtain employment as a labourer. During his time off on weekends, the cook would rush back to Macfarlane and report the number of Japanese personnel, equipment and gun emplacements, and the progress of work at the airfield. Given the low level of education and lack of experience that limited most Solomon Islanders' ability to provide precise numbers and describe modern artillery and other equipment, other islanders were encouraged to seek work with the Japanese so coastwatchers could compare information and obtain a more accurate report to be relayed up the intelligence line. To obtain accurate counts of personnel, Macfarlane instructed his team of scouts to watch as the Japanese lined up for food and estimate the length of the line. The estimates were far from exact, but sufficient enough to determine enemy strength at Lunga in early 1942. Coastwatcher and Australian veteran of World War I Ashton (Snowy) Rhodes and district officer Martin Clemens also sent their scouts to work for the Japanese forces at Lunga from their respective hideouts. Rhodes's scouts laboured at the Japanese airfield and bartered food while gathering what information they could on the progress of Japanese development around Lunga. Dressed as villagers, Clemens's policemen were sent to Tulagi, Gavutu and Tanambogo to gather information on enemy development. However, little was obtained from Clemens's initiative to spy on Tulagi since Japanese forces discouraged local visits to their camps (Feldt 1991: 112).

The quest for intelligence continued, however, as islanders masqueraded as willing civilian helpers. They would help Japanese soldiers to unload cargo and military equipment by day, slipping away into the jungle at night to report back their findings. Clemens reported that one of his scouts returned from a reconnaissance mission with unusually detailed intelligence. When Clemens asked how he could make so accurate a report, the scout replied, 'I wanted to know exactly what they got, so I helped them unload it' (COI 1946: 19). A similar intelligence-gathering method was used by Mostyn Kiokilo, one of Geoffrey Kuper's prominent scouts to whom the Allied forces owed a great debt. Mostyn often pretended to be a civilian, gathering the best fresh fruits and vegetables he could find and taking them to the Japanese seaplane base at Rakata Bay as gifts to Lieutenant Yoneda, commander of the base. His friendly approach earned him the trust of Yoneda, who willingly showed him gun emplacements and revealed the strength of his force. According to Walter Lord (1977: 166), 'Mostyn had won the confidence of Lieutenant Yoneda … and his information was regularly used by the Henderson Field bombers'. After each Allied bombing raid, Mostyn would return to the Rakata Bay camp to sympathise with Yoneda while assessing the damage caused by Allied bombers. This reveals how courageous and cunning scouts were.

Ordinary villagers also actively participated in intelligence gathering throughout Solomon Islands. Villagers who lived in coastal areas were expected to report any unusual sightings or events in their surrounding areas. Many Solomon Islanders provided invaluable assistance to Allied forces in this manner. It is possible that some forms of collaboration took place in circumstances where friendly relationships were developed between Japanese soldiers and islanders. However, there is no record of this occurring, except in the case of native medical practitioner George Bogese, who was captured by Japanese forces on Tulagi and forced to collaborate by translating Japanese notices to the local vernacular of his home island of Isabel.[3]

One of the notable stories of how intelligence was gathered by islanders was the story of Bingiti, a villager who led scouting activities around Nggela (Florida) Islands, 25 miles east of Guadalcanal and 35 miles west of Auki on Malaita. Despite this considerable distance of open ocean, Bingiti paddled his canoe from Nggela to Auki to report Japanese activities at Tulagi, or at times sent his fellow scouts to do the job. Bingiti and his men relayed detailed information that was of great assistance to Resident Commissioner Marchant at his headquarters in Auki, eager to know the situation at Tulagi. Clemens claimed that Bingiti's 'detailed intelligence was first class' (1998: 123). Here is an example from a report by Bingiti relayed by radio from Clemens to Marchant in Auki:

> Following is a reliable report, not rumour. Tulagi residency not occupied. Flag flies from resident commissioner's office which is main Jap control centre. Superior officials live there together with several clerks. The sentries on government wharf are the only guard on Island. Alarm sounded by whistle. Estimated that 500 Japs camped on Island. Estimate

---

3   See Laracy (1991). The tale of Bogese is discussed in Chapter 3 under 'Infliction of penalties'.

prepared by actual counting. One 'usual' [Kawanisi][4] anchored near government wharf, other five anchored at Gavutu where Jap garrison of similar number remain under flag erected on top of island. All European establishments round the harbour and within easy reach have been ransacked but are now no longer occupied. Japs have not treated Nggelese well and they will not now work for them. Every time they visit a village Japs haul out the villagers' trunks and boxes and pinch their clothing. Supplies of food are being obtained by menace of arms. Launch went to Auriligo plantation last Monday, but doubt whether they got any as all cattle were driven into the bush long ago. Nggelese are cooperating to the extent that they have been telling the Japanese that all white men have gone. As regards to same, Japs told natives that they were short of food and clothing and that they were coming to collect pigs, fowls and produce from their gardens. They also let it be known that they were short of fuel oil and petrol. No further news from practitioners to attend their wounded, of which there are large numbers. Japs told Nggelese to clear out and run away to another island as they would require all food that was being produced (Clemens 1998: 124).

Such information immensely assisted the coastwatchers and other Allied forces in assessing Japan's military strength and predicting its activities throughout Solomon Islands. It also provides an insight into indigenous people's relationships to the occupying Japanese force. Ill treatment of islanders by Japanese soldiers such as the demanding of food and property at the point of a gun was not the best approach to building a relationship with islanders. The coastwatchers were aware that islander knowledge was important for successful military operations on the islands. Hence, it was to the Allies' advantage that the Japanese troops on Nggela mistreated the islanders, for such ill treatment spurred the rise of anti-Japanese resentment among islanders. Elsewhere in Solomon Islands during the course of the war, resentment towards Japanese looting gardens and demanding food at gunpoint continued to spread among the local populace, to the extent that in Western District the population was entirely pro-Allied, which greatly enhanced the chances for survival of Allied personnel in enemy territory (Belshaw 1950: 142). This will be discussed in more detail in the next chapter.

---

4   Kawanisi was the name of a Japanese aircraft manufacturer during World War II, producing a range of flying boats and floatplanes. Islanders had insufficient knowledge to distinguish between different Japanese aircraft but were trained by coastwatchers to identify aircraft according to different countries. Therefore, it is possible that any floating aircraft belonging to Japanese forces would be called a *kawanisi*.

2. ISLANDERS AT WAR

One of the local scouts who sparked great admiration among Allied troops was Sergeant Major Jacob Vouza of the British Solomon Islands Defence Force. Vouza was a policeman who had just retired after serving on Malaita. Not long after he returned to his village on Guadalcanal, the Japanese landed on Tulagi. Being a respected figure in his village and having acquired the status of 'big man' from his work as a policeman, Vouza went to Aola on the north-east coast to visit district officer Clemens, offering his services and inquiring what he could do for his government. Clemens instructed Vouza to organise and facilitate the scouting network in his area, east of present-day Honiara. Vouza's arm of the scouting network functioned as effectively as that of any of the coastwatchers throughout the islands, up to and after the Americans landed on Guadalcanal. On 19 August 1942, Vouza brought an Allied pilot who had been rescued by his scouts to the United States Marines beachhead at Lunga. Because of his status as 'headman', Vouza was given a tour of the American camp at Lunga by the marine intelligence officer. To ensure that Vouza would be able to return to the camp without being accosted by Allied sentries, he was given an American flag to wave as a means of identification every time he approached the camp. He was also given a scouting assignment.

On his way, Vouza realised that carrying the American flag could be dangerous, so he decided to hide the flag in his village and recover it on his return from his mission. Vouza changed course to his village, but ran into a Japanese patrol and was immediately captured and interrogated. Vouza agreed to lead the Japanese troops to the Americans. Having toured the marine base at Lunga, he knew that his captors could not match their strength, so he decided that taking them there would be like leading them into a trap. But Vouza's condition was deteriorating as he had been bayoneted by the Japanese soldiers during interrogation. Vouza and his captors reached the marine lines at Lunga Point just after midnight on 20 August 1942, provoking a strong response from the Americans. The ensuing 'Battle of Tenaru' put the Japanese troops into disarray, which gave Vouza the opportunity to escape into the Allied perimeter where his life was saved by American field medics.[5]

---

5   John Innes, Guide to the Guadalcanal Battle Field (2012). Note that in published histories, Vouza was represented as being tortured by the Japanese and left to die, then struggling on his own to the American lines (see also Tregaskis 1943: 112–34). Vouza recalled that he led the Japanese to Lunga and, when shooting broke out between the two forces, he escaped into the American perimeter, badly wounded from Japanese interrogation (John Innes, *Guadalcanal Battlefield Tour* (DVD), 2012). A DVD copy of John Innes' documentary can be obtained from the Solomon Scouts and Coastwatchers Trust, Honiara.

Vouza's story is an example of the courage of local scouts, as well as the risks they took in order to gather intelligence for the Allies. Vouza's actions precipitated one of the bloodiest battles of the campaign (and one of the most costly for the Japanese). He received a number of medals from the Allies, including the Silver Star Medal and Legion of Merit from the United States and the George Cross from the United Kingdom.[6] In 1992, a monument was erected in his honour by the American Battle Monuments Commission; it stands at the entrance to the Royal Solomon Islands Prison at Rove in Honiara.

Search and rescue missions

For both the Japanese and Allied troops, survival in the tropical jungle environment under war conditions was nearly impossible. As Judith Bennett (2009: 15) wrote, 'the environment threatened strangers'. Almost half of the Allied servicemen who perished during the battle for the Solomons lost their lives to malaria, dysentery, dengue fever and other tropical diseases. However, the numbers were much higher among Japanese troops, who often starved because Allied forces inflicted damage on Japanese convoys. On Guadalcanal, the Japanese Lieutenant Akogina noted, 'I killed some ants and ate them, they really tasted good' (ibid.). Another Japanese soldier wrote in his diary before he died that 'there is no sympathy in the jungle' (ibid.). These descriptions signify the difficulty of surviving in the tropical environment, particularly for downed pilots and beached sailors.

Despite the slim chances that an Allied pilot or sailor had if they became stranded in enemy territory, their knowledge of the scouting network gave a major boost to their morale. Many of these pilots and sailors were rescued by islanders, some in very bad condition.

When American forces occupied Guadalcanal and Nggela, Japanese forces retreated north-west to New Georgia, the Treasury Islands and as far as Bougainville Island. But this movement did not mean they abandoned Henderson Field. The Japanese made several attempts to retake the airfield, resulting in fierce air and naval battles taking place in New Georgia and the surrounding waters. These battles resulted in many pilots and sailors on both sides having their planes shot down or ships

---

6   Inscriptions on Vouza's monument. Rove Police Headquarters, Honiara.

sunk. Most of those who survived found themselves left behind in enemy territory. However, search and rescue missions organised by coastwatchers and carried out by local scouts saw a number of Allied personnel returned to Guadalcanal to continue fighting. These search and rescue accomplishments have been mainly credited to coastwatchers and scouts, but ordinary villagers also shared in this endeavour. Indeed, although the network was coordinated by the coastwatchers, the bulk of the rescue efforts themselves were carried out by Solomon Islanders (COI 1946: 33).

At least 321 Allied airmen and 280 United States sailors were rescued behind enemy lines during the Solomon Islands Campaign (Feldt 1991: 153). Notable among those rescued was Lieutenant John F. Kennedy, who later became president of the United States, and his PT-109 (patrol torpedo boat) crew. On the night of 1 August 1943, Lieutenant Kennedy and PT-109, among 14 other PT boats, were sent on a reconnaissance mission to Blackett Strait, south of Kolombangara Island. The purpose of the mission was to guard the strait, and engage, disrupt and damage the 'Tokyo Express' should it navigate through 'the Slot' (New Georgia Sound) to reinforce the Japanese on Guadalcanal.[7] In the early hours of the morning, the Japanese destroyer *Amagiri* loomed out of the darkness only 300 yards from PT-109's starboard bow. Before Kennedy and his crew could launch a torpedo, the *Amagiri* rammed the PT-109, throwing Kennedy and his crew overboard. Patrick McMahon, the engineer of the boat, was badly burnt in the collision. The PT-109 crew were helpless in enemy territory; firing a flare to attract possible rescue was not an option. Their only chance of survival was to swim for the shore, over 3 miles from their current location. However, the chance of being found and rescued by a scout gave them hope of returning to base alive. Lieutenant Kennedy and his crew swam for the shore, towing their wounded comrades (Lord 1977: 255–75).

Four days after the crash, local scouts Eroni Kumana and Biuku Gasa — working under coastwatcher and Royal Australian Navy Sub-Lieutenant Arthur Evans who manned the coastwatching post at Kolombangara — found Kennedy and his crew. Kennedy was searching for a piece of paper to scribble a message to the nearest coastwatcher when Kumana gave him a coconut husk instead. Impressed by Kumana's resourcefulness, Kennedy

---

7   The 'Tokyo Express' was a nickname used by United States forces to refer to Japanese convoys, which often travelled though New Georgia Sound (also known as the Slot) towards the southern Solomons to deliver supplies and reinforcements to Japanese forces.

inscribed a message on the husk: 'NAURO ISL ... COMMANDER ... NATIVE KNOWS POSIT ... HE CAN PILOT ... 11 ALIVE ... NEED SMALL BOAT ... KENNEDY' (Figure 5; Gasa and Kumana 1988: 88).[8]

Figure 5: The coconut husk used by J.F. Kennedy during the war
Source: John F. Kennedy Presidential Library and Museum (MO63.4852).

Kumana and Gasa returned to Evans with the message. The rescue of Kennedy and his crew took place on the night of 7 August 1943; by the next morning, the PT-109 crew safely reached the United States base at Rendova. After the war, Kumana recalled Lieutenant McMahon's burns and mentioned that they dug a small hole and covered him in leaves from a *buni* tree. He recalled: 'When he saw us he stood up and shook

---

8   When Kennedy became president he kept the coconut husk on his desk in the Oval Office. It is now archived by the John F. Kennedy Presidential Library and Museum in Boston.

our hands and cried' (WPA 1988: 21–3).⁹ Biuku Gasa, the other scout, recalled that two of Kennedy's crew told them 'not to shake hands with the others since some of them were badly burnt from the collision' (ibid.: 33–9). It was only due to the practice of regular patrols that Kennedy's team were rescued in time since the condition of the crewmen wounded in the collision was rapidly deteriorating.

Guerrilla warfare

Another significant aspect of scouting was guerrilla warfare. Young island men won pride and achievement in a wide array of unconventional combat. The realisation that coastwatchers relied on their knowledge of the island environment enhanced these attitudes, and islanders' ability to masquerade as curious civilians became an asset to coastwatchers masterminding guerrilla actions against Japanese troops. Almost all Solomon Islanders who assisted in coastwatching activities found themselves engaged in guerrilla combat. One remarkable case was Donald Kennedy's Army, led by Sergeant William (Bill) Bennett of the British Solomon Islands Defence Force. The 'Army' comprised 28 scouts and a team of carriers (Figure 6). Bennett stated: 'every time a report came Kennedy and I would sit down at a table and plan what to do and how to do it … We only picked those [Japanese patrols] that we knew we could kill … If a Japanese patrol was beyond our capability to kill we just left them alone' (Bennett 1988: 141).

Bennett, who was heralded in published histories for his bravery as a scout, recalled an occasion when six Japanese soldiers with well-equipped radios arrived in Seghe. Scouts had reported sighting the Japanese patrol group and Allied forces had been trying to ambush them for several days to no avail. Bennett gathered 12 scouts and asked Kennedy for permission to hunt down the six Japanese. Permission was granted and a prize of a case of cigarettes was promised to the scouts if they caught the Japanese soldiers. Bennett recalled:

> We left at about five o'clock. It was not very far from where we were staying, only about a mile by canoe. We kept on walking and by six o'clock the next morning we were there. Then I sniffed the air and I could smell them because their body odour was very distinct in the jungle …

---

9   Eroni (Aaron) Kumana, still alive in 2013, maintained a relationship with the former United States president's family. He was also often visited by tourists and built a monument to honour his own war effort and friendship with JFK.

I walked slowly and quietly and directly ahead of me were the six soldiers. They were packing their belongings and were about to leave ... we shot them all. We buried them properly, took their guns, their radios, and documents. Kennedy was very happy. Then right away the big box of cigarettes arrived (Bennett 1988: 143).

Figure 6: Members of Donald Kennedy's coastwatching group ('Kennedy's Army') in training at Seghe Point, New Georgia, June 1943. Billy Gina stands over the man sighting his rifle
Source: Photo by Michael Currin, courtesy University of Hawai'i Hamilton Library collection.

Bennett recalled that his army of scouts accounted for over 100 Japanese killed and 82 captured without any losses on their side. The coastwatchers' tactic of giving rewards to islanders greatly aided in maintaining morale among indigenous people and promoting healthy competition among the islanders, with the added motivation of winning a prize for successfully performing a task. The reward of acquiring rifles from their victims seemed to be a particular lure for local participation in guerrilla skirmishes. In another remarkable event, Steven Vinale Zaku, a scout from Isabel Island under coastwatcher Geoffrey Kuper's command, recalled his experience of a guerrilla hunt for 25 Japanese aboard a barge at San Jorge Island. His party of scouts reached San Jorge shortly after the boat left, but they followed it until they reached Mufu village on Isabel where the Japanese unit stopped to revive. As Zaku recalled:

When morning came, we saw 6 men coming on patrol. They were coming ahead and we thought about capturing [them] because our orders said to do that. But the orders didn't say to take prisoners. The orders were to kill them but we thought about capturing them because if we shot them some of the others staying with the boat would hear the shots and come ready to fight. That's why we wanted to capture them so we could kill them quietly (Zaku et al. 1988: 158).

Zaku and his fellow scouts initiated a plot to wipe out all 25 Japanese. They first decided to invite a six-man Japanese patrol for some food. The plot was to launch an attack while the Japanese were eating. Zaku stated the Japanese wanted to hold on to their guns but Sergeant Tanisapa persuaded them to put their guns aside for the meal. While they were eating, another scout took all the guns and escaped. As soon as a signal was given, Zaku and his comrades attacked and killed the six Japanese soldiers. They then ambushed and killed the remaining soldiers as well. Zaku and his team engaged in a remarkable campaign of guerrilla fighting. Their exploits generated a significant mystery for Japanese forces and after the war resulted in a 1973 expedition to search for the missing 25 Japanese. Although the mystery of the never-recovered barge gave hope to the expedition team that there could be survivors, their search resulted in disappointment as none were found. Zaku's story, like those of other scouts who participated in guerrilla warfare, provides a glimpse into guerrilla activities during the campaign. Their stories have provided crucial explanations for missing Japanese units (*Pacific Islands Monthly* 1973: 6).

In a traditional society where a death was usually compensated for by reciprocal bloodshed, many Solomon Islanders, like Daniel Kalea, felt compelled to join the war. Daniel was from the highlands of Guadalcanal and a father of four children. His wife was killed by Japanese forces during operations on Guadalcanal in mid-1942. Daniel enlisted as a scout (Figure 7) and was earmarked to work alongside the United States Marine raiders on Guadalcanal. In traditional Solomon Islands societies, tribal fighting was very common. Although the influence of Christianity and the establishment of British administration over the islands had curbed traditional practices of warfare, traditional cultural attitudes were still engraved in people's minds. In the case of Daniel, whose wife was killed by an enemy on which he could take revenge with impunity, the opportunity to avenge his loss on Japanese troops was an easy choice. Driven by rage over his wife's death, Daniel engaged in his own private quest for vengeance in guerrilla skirmishes.

Figure 7: Daniel Kalea
Source: United States National Archives.

South Pacific Scouts

Besides the informal scouting network, some islanders also joined military units, particularly the South Pacific Scouts, which predominantly comprised Pacific islanders from Fiji, Tonga and the British Solomon Islands. Prior to Japan's invasion of the British protectorate headquarters at Tulagi, a defence force composed predominantly of Solomon Islanders was formed and trained by personnel of a detachment of the Australian Imperial Force manning a base at Tanambogo (Figure 8). The force consisted of a European commanding officer, a local warrant officer and 112 islanders of other ranks. Major Vivian Fox-Strangways, the commanding officer, had been in the Solomons for only a fortnight. He had been appointed resident commissioner for the Gilbert and Ellice Islands, but upon his arrival he found that the colony had been invaded by Japanese troops. From there, Fox-Strangways was commissioned to the rank of major and sent to administer the newly formed defence force at Tulagi. His task was to train islanders to use weapons that most of them had never seen before. But there was a problem: stocks of weaponry on hand were old and not sufficient to equip a military force. Fox-Strangways made a formal complaint to the British Solomon Islands Protectorate and gave suggestions for weaponry assistance (COI 1946: 10). His suggestions were never considered and the continual Japanese raids at Tulagi and the nearby islets of Gavutu and Tanambogo escalated, resulting in the complete evacuation of Fox-Strangeways's command. Even if his suggestions had been considered, his request for more weapons for his force of islanders would likely not have been granted. The Japanese assaults on Pearl Harbor and Singapore diverted Allied attention and Tulagi was of least concern at that time. On 2 May 1942, the Royal Australian Air Force and Australian Imperial Force detachment base at Tanambogo was evacuated and its equipment returned to Australia. The newly formed defence force was also dispersed but training was later reinforced elsewhere in the Solomons.

In spite of the failed attempt to form a defence force, the brief military training provided by Fox-Strangways had given the islanders involved basic knowledge in handling a gun. Although most of the islanders from the dispersed force returned to their villages, some attached themselves to coastwatchers as scouts and others later formed the nucleus (alongside Fijians and other Pacific islanders) of a guerrilla army — formally known to American forces as the 'South Pacific Scouts', to its members it was called the 'International Brigade', in a reference to the Spanish Civil War of the 1930s (COI 1946: 54).

Figure 8: Members of Donald Kennedy's coastwatching group ('Kennedy's Army'), wearing mostly captured Japanese helmets, in formation at Seghe Point, New Georgia, June 1943
Source: Photo by Michael Currin, courtesy University of Hawai'i Hamilton Library collection.

Some of the islanders who later become part of the South Pacific Scouts were initially recruited on Malaita to assist American forces in reconnaissance work on Guadalcanal. This group of Malaitan men was known as the 'service battalion' (Marchant 1943a). Colin Larsen, one of the few writers who mention this battalion, refers to it as the 'Dukwasi unit'.[10] The unit, according to Larsen (1946: 99), was reorganised and substantially reduced as it was evidently unable to operate effectively as a separate unit, hence needing to be attached to a better trained and organised unit. When attached to other units, it could be used effectively for scouting and patrol work.[11]

---

10 Dukwasi is a term in my native language of Kwara'ae that means 'wild jungle'. It is also the name of a village in central Kwara'ae on Malaita.
11 Although this was the reason for reorganising the unit, George Maelalo's (1988: 178) recollection indicates the unit served in frontline battle alongside the Fijians, Tongans and New Zealanders.

George Maelalo was among 22 Solomon Islands men attached to the 1st Reconnaissance Company, Fiji Guerrillas. This company was commanded by Captain Charlie Tripp, and the Solomon Islander unit was led by Lieutenant Len Barrow of the British Solomon Islands Defence Force. The unit fought alongside Allied forces in New Georgia and later in Bougainville as fighting shifted west of the British Solomon Islands Protectorate. In his recollection of events, Maelalo downplayed his considerable bravery when he volunteered for a mission to destroy a Japanese radar and radio installation on a hill at Sorokina in Bougainville. Maelalo recalled that some American and Australian soldiers attempted to blow up the radar but never returned from their mission. When his superiors called for a volunteer, Maelalo stepped forward with the intent of representing his comrades and proving his ability as a Solomon Islander soldier. He destroyed the radar, making way for Allied troops to capture one of the Japanese strongholds on Bougainville. While Maelalo claimed in his oral recollection that his choice to volunteer for the mission was to prove the ability of his fellow islanders and display their knowledge of the environment (Maelalo 1988: 178), it is worth noting that his motivation to volunteer reflects a common 'rite of passage' among young men in the traditional societies of Solomon Islands, an issue that will be discussed in the next chapter.

Maelalo's accomplishment shows that islanders who served in frontline units took the same risks that other Allied forces took, and suffered the same challenges that other units experienced in fighting throughout Solomon Islands and beyond. Maelalo recalled that on Bougainville the Islander Company worked tirelessly to build an airstrip for an airlift of dead and wounded soldiers: 'We built the airfield with our own bare hands. We dug trees with shovels and axes' (ibid.: 194). Of the 23 Solomon Islanders who served with the South Pacific Scouts, only seven, including Maelalo, were still alive when hostilities ended in 1945 (ibid.: 179). Despite Maelalo's actions, and the legacy of those islanders who sacrificed their lives for the Allied cause, their efforts have gone unrecognised for many years and have been submerged under the dominant narratives of outsider perspectives. This has influenced understandings of islanders' efforts in the war and the information that has been passed down into the contemporary Solomon Islands.

Communications and logistics

In any military campaign, effective communication is essential. This was the case between the coastwatchers and Allied forces in the Solomon Islands Campaign. To achieve effective communication over great distances, scouts were appointed in each major village to transmit information as quickly as possible. The process of communication in this sense can be classified into two categories: the approach to relaying unclassified information to coastwatchers, and the network of communication between coastwatchers that islanders facilitated. The indigenous approach was simple: if a Japanese patrol or unit was sighted in the bush, the information would be reported to the chief in the nearest village. The chief would swiftly send a scout or other able person on to the next village, and the pattern would continue until news reached the nearest coastwatcher. Scouts were instructed by coastwatchers in the manner of transmitting information. For relaying written letters and classified information among coastwatchers, a trusted scout would be assigned the responsibility. The ability of scouts to move through and between enemy lines at short notice to facilitate communication enormously aided coastwatching efforts and Allied operations throughout the British protectorate. Coastwatchers and Allied personnel were well aware of their reliance on local support of communications throughout the islands (Tadangoana 2011). Communication among coastwatchers was complicated in enemy-dominated territory, but was nevertheless maintained. Martin Clemens's network of communication was extended to every village under his administration along the coast of Guadalcanal. He recorded in his diary:

> every coastal village had formed a home guard section, which was responsible for reporting any enemy or strange activity along the coast ... Another important duty all villagers accepted — I could hardly force them to take it on — was feeding any of my chaps passing their way, and furnishing runners to pass on written messages. This service helped immeasurably to ensure that information reached me as soon as possible (Clemens 1998: 113–14).

Being in a foreign land during a war could generate insecurity and suspicion of indigenous allegiance. Clemens was aware that his life would be at stake if islanders chose to reveal his location to the Japanese or decided to switch allegiances. He incorporated village chiefs and headmen into his intelligence network. This aided his own peace of mind, and to ensure the reliability of the local communication system he passed a test message from one home guard section to the next, across his area of Guadalcanal from Aola as far as Rere in the east. The incorporation of traditional village leaders in the network was a significant aspect in the success of Clemens's intelligence gathering, and it proved to be a workable system among coastwatchers throughout the Solomon Islands (Figure 9).

Figure 9: Martin Clemens and his scouts (standing left to right: Daniel Pule, Martin Clemens, Andrew Langabaea; seated left to right: Olorere, Gumu, Chaparuka, Chaku)
Source: United States Marine Corps, National Archives (127-N-50505).

Clemens wrote in his diary that the response he got from his scouts was always prompt, and he acknowledged that 'there was little doubt my chaps were on the job' (Clemens 1998: 134). But an incident occurred towards the end of June 1942 that showed how islanders were risking their lives while running Clemens's communications. A scout arrived at Clemens's outpost at Paripao with a letter of complaint from Bishop Aubin at the Marist mission headquarters at Visale. Aubin feared that a rumour was circulating among the local population that he was pro-Japanese. Clemens replied to Aubin and sent his scout Chimi to deliver the letter. But Chimi was also instructed to spy on Japanese developments at Lunga while on his way. Chimi was aware that if he was caught by Japanese and they found he was carrying a letter, he would be killed. And, indeed, it was a task that almost claimed Chimi's life: he was spotted by the Japanese at Lunga as he sneaked between the neat rows of plantation coconuts; while being chased, he destroyed the letter. Although he managed to evade his pursuers by slipping away into a swamp (ibid.: 146), Chimi's story is one of a number of testimonials by islanders of the risks they took as messengers while ensuring the effective functioning of the coastwatching network.

In the western Solomons, John Kari's encounter with fallen American pilots exemplifies how ordinary civilians could become involved as messengers in a campaign not of their making. Kari was from Hopongo village on Rendova Island. In the 1920s, he attended Kokeqola Wesley United College at Munda on New Georgia. As a young, educated and ambitious man, he worked his way up to become a missionary teacher. His first encounter with Allied forces was when an American fighter plane was shot down by a Japanese Zero near his village at Hopongo. The two pilots survived the crash and swam ashore. Kari was the educated elite of his local society and one of the few islanders in his district who could speak English. Therefore, when the pilots were found, news reached him quickly and he approached the pilots in order to determine whether they were friend or foe. After a few questions, he concluded the pilots were Americans. But his guests were uncertain of his association with Allied forces, so he decided to assure them by showing a charter of a welfare society he had founded in 1930. Relieved and impressed by what they heard, the pilots donated US$30 to his initiative. But Kari could not imagine that the money presented to him would result in a three-month jail term in Seghe. News of the rescued pilots and the donation reached Donald Kennedy's coastwatching station at Seghe. Kari was called to bring the pilots to Seghe and, shortly after the pilots left for Henderson Field, Kari found himself in court for accepting a charity donation from the Americans. Kennedy may have viewed the generosity of Allied soldiers as a threat to colonial control over islanders. Therefore, detaining Kari would signal to other islanders that accepting gifts from Allied soldiers was not acceptable and would incur penalties. Kari recalled, 'I didn't get whipped but he [Kennedy] said I would have to stay at Seghe for 3 months' (Clemens 1998: 146). Kari's punishment was to remain at Seghe and work as a scout. He was then sent back to Hopongo with orders from Kennedy to set up a messenger post between coastwatchers Evans at Kolombangara and Horton at Rendova. People from Hopongo and nearby villages reported to him, and he would send messengers to report to Evans and Horton. Despite his unfair treatment, John Kari remained a reliable messenger who facilitated communication networks between Evans and Horton, and accommodated other stranded Allied personnel rescued by his fellow villagers. His gallant efforts earned him the United States Medal of Freedom, and were further recognised in a letter from the secretary of the navy in Washington DC:

> For exceptional meritorious conduct in the performance of service to the Government of the United States in effecting the escape of a Marine Corps Aviator and his air crewman who had been forced down off Baniata Point, Rendova Island, 1 November, 1942. Gallantly going to the rescue of the downed airmen in defiance of watchful Japanese garrisoned in the vicinity, Kari not only attended to the physical well-being of the two marines but guarded against detection by the Japanese while making detailed plans for the difficult journey by canoes and throughout the long and hazardous trip, Kari not only prevented their capture by Japanese forces but also was responsible for their return to a place of safety. His heroic conduct, fearless initiative and loyalty to Allied survivors of combat reflect the highest credit upon Kari and the friendly civilians of the islands who rendered valiant and unselfish service throughout this perilous mission (Laracy and White 1988: 104).

Like John Kari, Daniel Gua was also a student at Kokeqola College. He volunteered for scouting at Kennedy's request. He and his fellow villagers' job was to deliver letters to coastwatchers. He recalled:

> Every night we paddled. Down to Duke, Bilua, Simbo and Ranonga … many of the letters were from Seghe to Vonunu, where the minister there Sylvester, was the Coastwatcher too. This was before Josselyn came down from Tulagi to be the Coastwatcher. We took all the reports from headmen and these Coastwatchers in between and back and forth (WPA 1988: 87–94).

Other scouts were also involved as messengers. In an oral testimonial, Solomon Alu, a scout at Denggio in the western Solomons recalled that 'messages and letters went so fast … we had two boys on the shore, in case any messages came at night, they would run up the hill with them' (WPA 1988: 16–17). Scouts who were assigned to the communication routes were well aware of the urgency of their tasks. Micah Mae recalled his involvement as a sentry and messenger to Josselyn: 'We didn't sleep at night. When a letter came we would go' (ibid.: 20). The efforts of messengers did not go unacknowledged. Kennedy noted in his coastwatching report:

> Constant communication with both [Josselyn and Horton] was maintained, not only by teleradios, but also by native canoe patrols, and by this latter means mails and valuable sketches and maps were sent to Sehge to be picked up by Catalina aircraft from Halabo which began to land in Sehge channel in December (Kennedy 1943: 5).

The Solomon Islands Campaign became an Allied battle against two different opponents: the mighty Japanese Empire and the difficult environment. To those coastwatchers who remained behind enemy lines, it was a matter of surviving each day. But islanders knew their environment: it was their home. If anyone could navigate the tropical terrain, it would be the islander. Therefore, indigenous involvement in the coastwatching network became fundamental to its success. Two important ways that islanders supported the logistical mission were the movement of materials and supplies by canoes and carriers. Indigenous canoes and carriers provided not only a ready means of transportation of supplies between islands, among coastwatchers and across mountains, but also of delivering rescued Allied personnel to coastwatching posts and inserting patrol missions along coastlines (see Figure 10 for an example of the type of canoe (*tomoko*) that Solomon Islanders of Western Province used during the war). Islanders throughout the islands were actively mobile, to the great advantage of coastwatchers and Allied forces (Bennett 2009: 27).[12]

Guadalcanal district officer and coastwatcher Martin Clemens was among the few district officers who, of his own will, chose to remain in the protectorate as a coastwatcher during the war. He noted in his diary that he sent his men as far as Tulagi, travelling in small canoes (Clemens 1998: 44). Aided by indigenous navigation skills, these small canoes were used to travel great distances and saved many Allied lives. When describing the canoes, Donald Kennedy stated:

> the canoe used by the Solomon Islanders is cunningly built, but is not a plaything for the un-initiated. It's like a bicycle — whether it works or not depends entirely on the person riding it. The Islanders themselves travel blithely to and fro in these flimsy craft with the unthinking skill of a cyclist, steering their few inches of freeboard safely through rolling seas (COI 1946: 18).

---

12   See also Chapter 3 for discussion on the tropical island environment and diseases.

2. ISLANDERS AT WAR

Figure 10: Scouts of the western Solomons in a *tomoko* canoe
Source: United States National Archives.

Islanders were readily available along coasts in their canoes. Every time an aircraft was seen to be encountering difficulties, they would paddle out to sea for an immediate rescue. They were instructed by their coastwatchers to rescue both Allied and Japanese soldiers. The rescue of United States Navy flyer Lieutenant J.G. Steussey was an example of such invaluable assistance. After being shot down by a Japanese Zero, Steussey's bomber crashed and he found himself paddling his tiny life raft to a strange shore. Remarkably, an islander sitting in his canoe saw him and swiftly towed him to shore; if he was spotted by a Japanese aircraft, his chances of survival would have been unlikely. Steussey related that islanders bandaged his wounds, fed him hot sweet potatoes and covered him with a blanket. He was then carried on a stretcher across the island to where he was transported back to Guadalcanal. Steussey recalled that 'it was a long way over rough country' (COI 1946: 32).

The stealthy operation of coastwatchers on and between rugged mountainous islands necessitated effective mobility and intelligence gathering. The teleradio type 3B or 3BZ (Figure 11) that coastwatchers used to transmit intelligence was designed for the Flying Doctor Service of Australia. It was designed to suit tropical conditions but was very heavy to carry. It operated by a six-volt battery with a separate charging motor and weighed over 100 kg. It required 12 to 16 islanders to carry it every time a coastwatcher relocated his camp (Clemens 1998: 40).

Figure 11: AWA Teleradio 3BZ used by coastwatchers during the war
Source: Australian War Memorial (P01035.006).

Teleradios were not the only load to be borne when operating behind enemy lines. After Japanese occupation of Tulagi, Clemens's scouts reported there were continuous visits to neighbouring Guadalcanal by Japanese forces. Clemens realised it would be a grave risk to remain at the administrative station at Aola and decided it was time to move inland. On 19 May 1942, he evacuated Aola, eight days before Japanese troops landed at Tenaru on Guadalcanal. To ensure a lighter load for his carriers, Clemens paid as many workers as he could with the government's silver in his possession, but the load remained heavy. Clemens needed as many carriers as he could get to quickly shift the entire station inland to Paripao, so he sent word around to the villages for men who would be willing to do the job. Labouring was not voluntary — islanders expected payment, and Clemens was well aware of this. He knew his life depended on his reputation among islanders, and one way to maintain goodwill was to ensure any labour recruits be immediately compensated with good wages. By 19 May 1942, Clemens had assembled 190 carriers and departed Aola, leaving only his trusted scout Sergeant Andrew Langabaea to run the scouting network in the area. He took everything he would need to maintain not only a coastwatching station but a skeleton administration as well, to uphold morale and maintain the government presence among local people. Among Clemens's possessions was the district officer's safe, which Clemens thought was too heavy to carry. So he emptied its load of silver coins and transferred them to a travelling safe, which still required four people to carry (Clemens 1998: 121). The safe was reported to contain £800 worth of silver (Lord 1977: 19).

But Clemens did not remain at Paripao for long. In early June 1942, Japanese troops landed on Guadalcanal in force to begin construction of the airfield. Again, Clemens and his scouts and carriers retired further inland for safety. At the Burns Philp rubber plantation at Lavoro on Guadalcanal, coastwatcher Rhodes also evacuated inland with his 24 scouts and carriers, while Macfarlane and Hay abandoned their position at Gold Ridge and moved south to Bombedea. These evacuations took place from early to mid-July during early Japanese developments on Guadalcanal.

In the western Solomons, similar relocations occurred. Solomon Alu, a scout, recalled the relocation of coastwatcher McKennon's post from the vicinity of Mundimundi to a vantage point at Denggio. Alu remembered:

> We carried everything up that hill. Those batteries for the radio were heavy to carry in the bush. We took roofing iron to build their house … we took iron from the Mundi house and from a house at Vatoro to make three houses, theirs [coastwatchers], ours [scouts] and a third for the radio itself. I think we had 27 Solomon Islanders up there (WPA 1988: 16–17).

After the United States Marines landed on Guadalcanal in August 1942, islanders on Guadalcanal, from Malaita and elsewhere in the protectorate, were recruited in large numbers to form the Native Labour Corps, while a few locals were incorporated into military units as artillery carriers. Coastwatchers became the recruiting agents for islanders during the war. Published records mostly mention Solomon Islanders only in passing, unlike the famous 'fuzzy wuzzy angels' of Papua New Guinea whose effort in the war become widely celebrated in written histories.[13] Islanders were regarded as onlookers more than participants during the war, a viewpoint that will be discussed throughout the next chapters. Despite these representations, local oral recollections, photographs and testimonials from many of the combatants who served in the campaign indicate otherwise. A photograph taken on 10 October 1942 at Aola station, Guadalcanal, features one of Clemens's trusted scouts, Selea, and a group of local carriers assembled with Lieutenant Colonel Hill and his troops prior to an attack on the Japanese garrison at Gorobusu (Figure 12).

Figure 12: Scout Salea (centre) and ammunition carriers (right) with Colonel Hill's troops at Aola, Guadalcanal, 10 October 1942
Source: United States Marine Corps.

It is evident from the photo that islanders were enlisted to carry boxes of ammunition for the fighting force. This task does not feature prominently in the historiography as an islander contribution to frontline combat, yet it showed an active inclusion of islanders in frontline efforts with Allied troops. A similar image highlights islanders carrying crates along a trail on

---

13   See also the film *Angels of War* (Pike et al. 1982).

the grassy plains of Guadalcanal (Figure 13). The photograph, produced by the United States Marine Corps during the war, indicates these islanders were carrying supplies. The original caption stated: 'Lieutenant Colonel Carlson's supply train winds across the grass plains on their return from a month-long expedition against the Japanese'.

Figure 13: Lieutenant Colonel Carlson's supply train, Guadalcanal
Source: United States Marine Corps.

However, the expectation of paid wages among islanders for any means of involvement was problematic for both the coastwatchers and fighting units, and local carriers were not always completely dependable. In a message to Clemens, Macfarlane complained that he had no carriers to assist in his evacuation inland and requested Clemens to send some of his carriers to do the job. Meanwhile, on 9 January 1943, 130 Guadalcanal carriers who were recruited by coastwatchers to assist the United States 147th Infantry Battalion (170 men) on a patrol to Vurai in the interior of Guadalcanal demanded an increase in their wages. Five days into the job, carriers engaged in a strike for higher wages, which resulted in the arrest of their leader (Laracy and White 1988: 141). It is fair to say that islanders were aware the tasks they were assigned to perform were significant to the success of the patrols, and the increase in money circulating among villagers when the Americans arrived increased islander expectations of higher wages when recruited to guide patrols or as carriers. Despite these complexities, the efforts islanders rendered to the Allied cause in terms of logistical support were indisputably significant.

Labour corps

When United States forces captured Guadalcanal and began to penetrate the western Solomons, fierce battles ensued. But the need for labour was not of immediate concern until three months after the occupation of Guadalcanal. On 30 November, the protectorate's resident commissioner, William Marchant, officially endorsed recruitment for a Solomon Islands Labour Corps. The first cohort of islanders was recruited on Malaita and included six groups of 25 men each. These groups of recruits formed the majority of the first 200 native labour corpsmen who enlisted as privates and sergeants and were stationed at Lunga.[14]

Among these first 200 labourers was Isaac Gafu of Malaita. In his oral recollection, Gafu listed the labourers' tasks as 'unloading and carrying cargo, building airfields, and spraying the ponds to keep down malaria … also carrying ammunition for the army' (Ngwadili and Gafu 1988: 207). In early 1943, the labour corps sections at Lunga were assigned to the Koli, Lunga, Tenaru and Kukum bases. Gafu, assigned to Koli base, recalled the labourers' duties as guarding the fighter strip, loading ammunition and carrying cargo. He also describes an assortment of other tasks, stating 'some went to do laundry, some went to work on lumber, and some went to work on gasoline' (ibid.: 209). Jonathan Fifi'i also affirmed labourers' contribution to the war effort by stating:

> Our work was to unload shells … we unloaded bombs and stacked them in piles. And we also unloaded cargo. We handled an incredible amount of cargo! All the food that they [the Americans] ate. We cleared trails for the Americans to travel on to reach the Japanese and fight with them. And we were bearers, carrying ammunition and guns and all the gear for the men. We carried them along, with the Marines when they were going to fight (Fifi'i 1988: 223).

Labourers were exposed to continual Japanese raids on Allied bases at Lunga and the vicinity. Gafu described how the brutality of modern warfare was experienced when 11 islanders were killed and nine wounded in a bombing raid on 26 January 1943 at Lunga. To Gafu, the horror of this incident did not fade as his memory aged. He recalled that 'when

---

14   Although military operations in the Solomons diminished from early 1943, Native Labour Corps recruiting continued to provide workers for clean-up operations, and by 1944 the corps had recorded a total recruitment of 3,710 labourers.

you hear the air raid signal, you must go into the foxholes. You must not stay above ground or you will die' (Ngwadili and Gafu 1988: 208). In narrating the incident of 26 January 1943, he reiterated:

> one day the Japanese bombed us and killed 60 of our people … every one of us quickly ran into the foxholes. The people who were killed by the bombs stayed above ground. They did not run into foxholes quickly enough (Ngwadili and Gafu 1988: 208).[15]

The bombing raid stirred up fear among the labourers. Gafu commented on their reactions after the bombing as they fled their camps at Lunga in the grip of fear and shock: 'We ran away and did not care about work. We were afraid and stayed in the bush' (ibid.: 208). In a telegram to the high commissioner of the British protectorate, Resident Commissioner Marchant reported a refusal to work after the bombing, predominantly among Malaita labourers (Marchant 1943b). These reactions contrast with a description in a booklet compiled by the Central Office of Information for the Colonial Office in 1946. Commenting on islanders' contributions in the war, the booklet characterises islanders' reactions to bombing as 'displeasure rather than panic' (COI 1946: 34). In comments on islander responses to the 26 January bombing incident, it stated:

> Although this terrifying and entirely novel experience had a momentary effect on their morale, not one of the new recruits sought release from his undertaking to serve the Corps. Instead, they quietened their jangling nerves by digging extra foxholes (COI 1946: 34).

This assessment does not quite capture the nature of the experience as related by Gafu.

The role of women

Although direct involvement of islanders in the war was entirely among males, this left a gap in local communities. A shift in the balance of gender power occurred due to the absence of most men from their villages. As will be discussed in the next chapter, one of the lures for local involvement in

---

15 Note the discrepancies between Gafu's figure of 60 casualties and the officially reported 11 deaths and nine wounded. This is perhaps due to an exaggeration or possibly a figure determined under trauma of the event. The official figure is from the resident commissioner's report to the high commissioner.

the war was an increase in wage rates for islanders. This resulted in men migrating from their villages to seek labour opportunities at military bases, particularly on Guadalcanal and in the western Solomons (Figure 14).

Figure 14: Makira women and children watch as men from their island leave for labour corps work with the Allies on Guadalcanal, June 1943
Source: United States Navy, United States National Archives.

In the patrilineal societies of Malaita, the social structure was interrupted when large numbers of men migrated from their villages in search of paid labour. As David Gegeo documents for the Kwara'ae region, 'women became more active in village leadership, taking on new roles' (1991: 31). But Gegeo also reports that, at one stage, a group of Kwara'ae women 'marched to government headquarters to demand that the Kwara'ae men who had been recruited for war service be returned to Malaita' (1991: 31). This incident indicates the courage women summoned in the absence of their males to demand the government's attention. A comparable example of women's active participation in traditional leadership due to the absence of men can be seen in the wartime experiences of the people of Pohnpei, in the Caroline Islands of Micronesia. Although Pohnpei was not a centre of military activity as Guadalcanal was, most of the able-bodied men were recruited by Japanese military administrators for labour in Rabaul and elsewhere in the Pacific. In July 1943, over 170 Pohnpei men from Kitti were recruited and sent to Kosrae as labourers. According to researcher Suzanne Falgout, who studied wartime experiences in Pohnpei, 'Kitti women had been left behind to care for their families, farmsteads, and community' (Falgout 1991: 124).

On islands like Guadalcanal where there was direct confrontation between Japanese and the Allies, women sometimes played an active role in protecting their men and the coastwatchers. Festus Butoa, an elder from Paripao who estimated he was about 12 years old during the war, recalled a time when the women of his village lured a few Japanese into a house with fruits and vegetables and kept them engaged while sending a warning to the scouts to seek shelter in the jungle (Butoa 2015).

On Malaita, as my grandmother recalls, all the women, children and elderly men of her village fled inland during the initial period of fighting on Guadalcanal and Tulagi. Most of the able-bodied men of the village were called by the 'government' to gather in Auki. For some families, both the father and oldest son left the village. Although everyone in the village looked out for each other, things were not the same. Women's responsibilities doubled as they became the only guardian of the family in the absence of men (Ngwae'hera 2015). Such situations stretched traditional norms of the roles played by women, requiring them to fill the gaps left by their male counterparts, both within individual households and in the community.

Conclusion

Islanders were not bystanders in the war but active participants. They were recruited as guides for military patrols, they infiltrated, observed and reported on the Japanese, they rescued personnel; they were the primary (and often the only) communication link between coastwatchers, they provided the manpower that kept the logistical side of the campaign moving and they actively engaged in combat in several different units and modes of fighting. These varied contributions significantly aided the Allied victory in the Pacific War. Local recollections make it clear that the dangers endured by Solomon Islanders were no less than those faced by foreign troops. Islanders displayed great courage, and many showed great strength and skill in difficult circumstances. Despite the hardships and losses they endured, Solomon Islanders overwhelmingly remained true to the Allied cause until the end of the war in 1945. The complex reasons for this will be examined in the next chapter.

3
Why Support the Allies?

The positive attitude of Solomon Islanders towards Allied forces during the Pacific War has attracted considerable speculation in the literature, with the overwhelming majority of commentators simply representing islanders as 'loyal natives'.[1] In a section on the British Solomon Islands Protectorate in his book *Return to Paradise*, James Michener compared the different perspectives that American troops had of islanders in Papua New Guinea and Solomon Islands. Although Papua New Guineans were observed to be more industrious than their neighbours in the British Solomon Islands, one thing that American troops could not deny was the 'loyalty' of Solomon Islanders during the war. Michener (1951: 185) states:

> on British islands not one white man was betrayed. Not one. The fidelity of Solomon Islanders was unbelievable. Hundreds of Americans live today because these brave savages fished them from the sea, led them through Jap lines and carried them in their canoes to safety.

This romanticised representation of wartime indigenous peoples is not unique to Solomon Islanders. In Papua New Guinea, the contributions of indigenous peoples as stretcher bearers, carriers, riflemen and soldiers has created the myth of the 'fuzzy wuzzy angels' in Australia (Hereniko 1999: 144). As historian Hank Nelson (2006: 136) noted, 'the "boy" had become the fuzzy wuzzy angel'.[2] However, Nelson (1978), Emma

---

1   These authors address islander roles in the Allied war effort on Guadalcanal and elsewhere in the British Solomon Islands Protectorate: Clemens (1998), Feldt (1991), Lindsay (2010) and Lord (1977).
2   'Boy' was a term used for Melanesian men of all ages during the colonial period.

Rogerson (2012) and others (e.g. Riseman 2010) have argued that these representations are far from the reality of islander experiences. Issues such as the method of recruiting islanders for labour used by the Australian and New Guinea Administrative Unit and the manner in which labourers were treated have proven otherwise. Nelson wrote:

> ANGAU officers and police entered villages, 'lined' the people, gave a 'pep' talk, and convinced most men that they must endure hard work, danger and separation from home. When villagers showed signs of resistance, the police seized traditional valuables, began eating the household foods and threatened to rape the women and recruit young boys unless deserters gave themselves up and able-bodied men agreed to go away as labourers. (Nelson 1978: 182–3)

In the British Solomon Islands Protectorate, recruitment of islanders was generally voluntary yet of a complex nature. When oral histories and other documentation are investigated, a number of issues emerge that help to explain more fully the complexities of the motivation behind the cooperation of islanders with the Allied forces during the Solomon Islands Campaign. Among the factors considered in this chapter are obligation, fear, curiosity and adventure, the lure of rising wages as Allied demand for labour increased, the relationship to Britain as a colonising power and the differing experiences of encounters with 'friend' and 'foe' during the war. Exploring these various motivations, it becomes clear that Solomon Islanders' participation in the war was more complex than the common representation of simple loyalty to the Allied cause.

Obligation — cultural attitudes and tradition

In 1893, in the process of regulating the illegal labour recruitment or 'blackbirding' of islanders, Great Britain declared a protectorate over Solomon Islands. Although islanders had come into contact with European explorers, traders and missionaries as early as the 1500s, little was known by the outside world about their way of life, social structures and practices. Information that would aid in implementing administrative policies was lacking, and the administrators of the protectorate were strangers to the indigenous inhabitants of the islands (Belshaw 1950: 23, 38–9). A lack of cross-cultural understanding contributed to the British colonisers' view of islanders as 'savage', 'uncivilised' and in need of a transformative cultural, moral and technological education. For their part, islanders were dazzled by their encounters with British ships, guns, tinned foods and other manufactured goods. Over time, such encounters resulted in islanders accommodating the colonisers' technologically superior culture. The supposedly superior 'Western' culture projected its dominant ideology, informing and sometimes dictating the everyday affairs of indigenous subjects. This was due to the method in which it was channelled into the society, and the perceptions of Solomon Islanders attributing prestige to the colonial authorities. Hence, to understand the extent to which Solomon Islanders felt a sense of obligation to assist Allied forces, it is appropriate to discuss the nature of prestige in the traditional leadership systems of Solomon Islands societies and how this influenced attitudes towards colonial administration.

There is a deeply held notion of respect for authority in the cultural make-up of Solomon Islanders and other Melanesians, which is a driving force in the nature of their sense of obligation to anyone with high status in traditional society. Take, for instance, the level of prestige a 'big man', chief or elder attains, the authority he possesses and the respect he commands. Big men express their authority by sponsoring ceremonial activities that attract the admiration of their kin and community, displaying their ability to appear as someone worthy of respect (Allen 1984: 23–4). However, the status of big man is not a political title. As Marshall Sahlins (1963: 290) famously pointed out, it is merely 'an acknowledged standing in interpersonal relations'. A big man's command is influential only within his community, and beyond that his reputation is known with diminishing influence over space and time. Although he does not use physical force to command respect, due to his standing within his society his admirers and followers often feel an obligation to submit to his commands. In his study of the Kapauku people of New Guinea, Leopold Pospisil (1958: 81) described this merit and relation-based Melanesian social structure, stating 'their obedience to the headman's decision is caused by motivations which reflect their particular relations to the leader'. The leader (big man or headman) 'must be prepared to demonstrate that he possesses the kinds of skills that command respect — magical powers, gardening prowess, mastery of oratorical style, perhaps bravery in war and feud' (Sahlins 1963: 291).[3]

---

3   It is also appropriate to mention here that those who obtained some form of Western education can be also classed as big men. The knowledge they acquired from formal education equipped them with skills that were foreign in a traditional society. See also Lindstrom (1984).

This social status of the big man becomes an important consideration when dealing with administration of indigenous affairs by the colonial authority (Kennedy 1946: 168–70). An eventual understanding by administrators of how local social structures functioned in the protectorate set a foundation for the war effort. When Japan occupied Solomon Islands, big men were immediately ushered into the war effort by district officers (who were also coastwatchers) as scouts, guides, carriers and labourers. The big men's immediate appearance alongside Allied forces indicated to the rest of the local population which side they ought to support.

Perceptions of the superiority of the white race, due to the skills and tools they brought, and the power of their medicine, appealed to islanders. It attracted their respect and enhanced a sense of obligation to subject themselves to these forms of supremacy. The esteem in which the islanders held the white coloniser did not indicate a breakdown of the prestige they attached to their traditional leaders, but it distorted the hierarchy by placing foreign authority figures above traditional leadership structures. The position of local leaders shaped how information was transmitted into society as well as how the colonial authorities executed initiatives. In other words, the British administration understood the functions of hierarchy in Solomon Islands society and manipulated them to the advantage of their cause. For instance, Eric Feldt described how coastwatchers Josselyn and Keenan on Vella Lavella organised a local scouting network and placed the chief of the island in command of the force:

> Bamboo [the chief] continued to administer native affairs on the island, advised by Josselyn who, however, kept in the background so that no native, resentful of an adverse decision in a civil matter, should be tempted to betray him in revenge (Feldt 1991: 243).

On Guadalcanal, district officer Martin Clemens had a 'pep talk' with the Marau district headmen in which he instructed them to relocate inland as soon as Japanese forces landed in the area. Clemens feared any contact with Japanese troops would reveal coastwatchers' locations; persuading locals to evacuate coastal villages would minimise the likelihood of contact with enemy troops. As soon as this instruction was agreed upon by the Marau headmen, it was passed on to all other headmen on the island as to what was expected from them (Clemens 1998: 89). Elsewhere in the Solomons, the same channel for transmitting information to the local population was used by district officers, coastwatchers and missionaries. Effectively, the local societal structure was used to the advantage of the Allied cause.

Feelings of obligation as a result of good social relationships

The administration of colonial Solomon Islands involved the collaborative efforts of missionaries and colonial administrators. Each could not accomplish much without the other. Despite different approaches to local affairs taken by the government and missionaries, both endeavoured to achieve a common goal, which was to deliberately 'transform' and even to 'revolutionise' the lives of islanders (Belshaw 1950: 44–7). By 1940, five church denominations — Roman Catholic, Anglican, South Seas Evangelical, Seventh-day Adventist and Methodist — had established and gained momentum in Solomon Islands. In some coastal villages where islanders encountered more than one Christian denomination, proselytism was common and local customs in these areas diminished (Osifelo 1985).[4] Hence, the transition to Christianity from 'paganism' witnessed a shift of prestige from pagan gods and spirits to the Christian god, but not a total elimination of the former. The functionality of local religion was altered by the introduced Christian notion of divine lineage: that all of humanity was created by God who, in this sense, is the common ancestor of all tribal groups. This did not lead to a total breakdown of the political boundaries of tribal sects, but Christian values became so widely accepted that they reduced tribal boundaries through a world view that unified all of humanity by asserting a common relationship with a single god. Therefore, the respect that was formerly demanded by traditional interlocutors to ancestral gods was now commanded by Christian elites. This contributed to islanders' allegiance to Allied troops during the war (Osifelo 1985: 1–6).

In early 1942, when Japan began its daily raids on Tulagi, the British colonial government called for the immediate evacuation of the expatriate community in the protectorate. But not all expatriates evacuated, and among those who remained were many missionaries. Some denominations like the Seventh-day Adventists evacuated all its missionaries. But for the South Seas Evangelical Mission, all but five of its missionaries

---

4   In this personal biography, Osifelo repeatedly described his family's movement from one church to another. His parents initially converted to Anglicanism, were then baptised into the South Seas Evangelical Church and his mother later converted to the Catholic Church. His father, on the other hand, stopped attending church after his second marriage (which was considered a sinful act of adultery in the South Seas Evangelical Church). Osifelo later reconverted to Anglicanism after his marriage to a pagan woman.

nominated to remain on Malaita. In the western Solomons, only three of the Methodist missionaries (including a female, Sister Merle Farland), remained at their posts.

However, almost all missionaries of the Catholic and Anglican churches refused the government's order for evacuation and remained in the protectorate to continue their religious duties. Although some missionaries maintained neutrality during the war, most were later absorbed into the coastwatching network and organised the local scouting network in their respective localities (Laracy 1988: 32).

This refusal to evacuate earned the missionaries admiration and gratitude from indigenous people. Their choice to remain in the islands was encouraged by denominational traditions. As Sister Merle Farland of the Methodist Mission wrote in her diary, the evacuation of missionaries was 'not consistent with Christian service' (Farland, February 1942: 36) and could be seen as abandonment. It could also inflict a moral defeat on the church and destroy the foundation that had been established in the protectorate over years. Farland was convinced that her choice to remain in the protectorate when Japan invaded would help maintain confidence in the mission. She described the reaction of islanders:

> They seem very glad for us to stay, tho' they do not want us to be in danger. It hurt them greatly to feel that the white staffs were deserting them without even putting the case before them, or stopping to plan for things with them. Clarrie Leadley left a letter here [at Patutiva] for Paul Havea telling him they were 'going away so that they would not die' but for them [islanders] to 'be courageous and carry on the work' (Farland, February 1942: 37).

Farland also indicated in her diary that George Hili, a teacher and ex–hospital boy, pointed out to her that 'while there was a white person in charge of hospital work, the natives would keep their confidence in the medical boys as teachers, but without one, the work would suffer badly' (Farland, February 1942: 36). The point made by George Hili not only shows the admiration towards white missionaries but also reflects the prestige they obtained among the indigenous population and their status in the social structure of the local societies they had influenced.

For missionaries like Father Emery de Klerk, a Catholic priest stationed at Tangarare on Guadalcanal, the refusal to evacuate also had a personal dimension. Father de Klerk was from Holland and had lost all contact with his family after Nazi Germany's advance into western Europe. Since Japan was a member of the Axis powers,[5] de Klerk saw an opportunity to avenge the injustice inflicted on his family by the dictatorship of Hitler. He became one of the missionaries who actively participated in the coastwatching network. On 3 January 1943, Father de Klerk was given an American commission by United States Army General Alexander Patch, for which he resigned his British commission. Harold Cooper wrote that 'de Klerk had a little Navy of his own, consisting of the ten-ton schooner "Kokorana" loaned to him by the government for the duration of his service with the armed forces' (Cooper 1945). Again, the courage of those missionaries who remained in Solomon Islands during the war, despite their personal motivations, certainly aroused the admiration of indigenous peoples. Hugh Laracy (1988: 32) rightly pointed out it 'helped ensure a high level of indigenous support for the Allied cause'. And, indeed, it built goodwill towards Allied troops throughout Solomon Islands.

It is not surprising that islanders admired the dedication of those missionaries who remained behind as leaders. Although locals did not want the missionaries to risk their lives, there was a mutual sense of fighting for a common cause to liberate Solomon Islanders from the Japanese Empire. In an interview conducted by Peter Crowe (1987), Bill Bennett, a local veteran of the British Solomon Islands Defence Force, described missionaries' tasks during the campaign somewhat romantically as 'bible in the right hand and bush knife in the left'. The courage of those missionaries who remained during the war considerably strengthened the sense of spiritual faith and loyalty of indigenous people among the confusion of hostilities.

The use of propaganda

Prior to the Japanese occupation of Solomon Islands, district officers travelled from island to island giving instructions on what was expected of the local population if Japan invaded. Along with these instructions, there was also the dissemination of propaganda on Japanese troops, regarding Japanese behaviour, morality and their intention to conquer indigenous lands. The use of land as a subject of propaganda was itself enough to

---

5   The Axis powers were founded in principle by Germany, Italy and Japan in the mid-1930s. These countries became the major opponents of the Allies during World War II.

influence the attitude of local elders. Land is a culturally fundamental issue that often leads to conflict within and between different cultural groups in Solomon Islands, and there is a strong sense of identification with it. Land is an important asset and the prospect of a stranger taking it away by force is culturally unacceptable. So the inclusion of land issues in Allied propaganda was likely to have a great impact on indigenous people's perspectives. In early 1942, Dick Horton, district officer and predecessor to Martin Clemens at Aola on Guadalcanal, toured his district and met with the elders of each village he visited, giving them instructions and spreading propaganda on Japanese troops. In his book *Fire Over the Islands*, Horton lays out the message that was delivered to the indigenous population:

> They [the Japanese] have bad men leading them; evil men who want more power and land. They have conquered many places to the north and killed and shamefully treated men and women. If they come here, none of us will be safe. We will fight them together but we must fight them in the way I will tell you. First, you must keep away from them and watch them — no one must talk to them. You must make new villages and gardens in the hills which are hidden and the tracks to them must be difficult to find. If the Japanese comes to your old village they must find nothing. You must bring me news of what they do and where they are. I will be somewhere in the Island and the work of Government will go on. I know you are faithful and loyal and, until we bring in our friends [the Americans] to help us, this is the best way we can help each other defeat the enemy (Horton 1970: 10–11).

It did not take long for such messages to reach every household, and the fear of what possible horrors the Japanese might inflict mounted even before there was any local contact with Japanese troops. Fear continued to escalate as the islanders watched planters and missionaries desert their homes and flee to Tulagi for evacuation. By early March 1942, Clemens noted in his diary that a crowd of headmen from all over Guadalcanal assembled around his desk at the district office in Aola in apprehension, eager to know what was going on. Clemens wrote:

> What could I say to them? I had taken over the district only three days earlier. The headmen had heard that my predecessor, Dick Horton, had gone; now the only other European on the station had orders to go. Terrified of what the Japanese might do to them and their families, they wanted to know that I would not desert them. And there we were, undefended, with the Japs flying over us to bomb the RAAF advance post on Tanambogo Island, nineteen miles away. What to do? I puffed on my

pipe and scratched my chin … 'if you stick with me, someone someday will come and save us, and everything will be all right' … Feeble though it was, that pledge was the basis for the tremendous show put up by the people of Guadalcanal during the dark days that followed (Clemens 1998: 31).

In Western District, district officer Donald Kennedy spread the same message and instructions as Horton and Clemens on Guadalcanal. Kennedy noted he visited villages and explained to headmen and elders the sorts of behaviour expected of islanders in the event of enemy invasion. Islanders were instructed to avoid the enemy and briefed on how to report information in the event of war. Nathan Oluvai recalled that even before the war 'we knew the Japanese were the enemy' (WPA 1988: 1). Kennedy reported soon after the war that 'the natives entered readily into all the plans and offered their services, their food supplies and their canoes without demur' (COI 1946: 13).

Infliction of penalties

Although islanders accepted the message spread by the district officers, they did not do so out of unquestioning loyalty to the administration. The instructions given to indigenous peoples dictated expected behaviours and norms of conduct and behaving otherwise could lead to penalties for the responsible individuals. In most instances, and as seen later during the campaign, islanders feared the consequences of disobeying orders from 'white masters' far more than the risks of combat. As in the Australian colonial territories of Papua and New Guinea, the inhabitants of Solomon Islands were subjected to the standard white colonial perceptions influenced by racial attitudes and feelings of dominance over 'primitive' populations (Silata 1988: 63–9).

Although coastwatchers depended entirely upon the indigenous population to carry out their duties during the war, there was little leniency in dealing with native affairs, especially in the infliction of penalties for minor offences. Forms of penalties included corporal punishment, loss of wages and hard labour. Different district officers employed their own strategies in handling offences of various natures. Martin Clemens indicated in his diary that offenders brought to him by chiefs were used as labourers and turned out to be resourceful during his coastwatching stint (Clemens 1998: 114). Despite the fact that these penalties were of a correctional nature and useful from the perspective of colonial officers, to islanders they became a force for coercing them to perform to the expectations of colonial 'masters'. Local scout Bill Bennett, second-in-command to district officer Kennedy, boldly stated in an interview conducted by journalist Peter Crowe that 'there is a system that you gotta bow down to the master and do as the master say … we're told what to do and even before the war come we're told what to do' (Crowe 1987). Scout Alfred Bisili told Crowe 'the war is nothing to do with Solomon Islanders; we're forced by the British officers to do scouting', re-emphasising Bennett's statement (ibid.). A similar statement was also made by scout Nathan Oluvai of Western Province, who recorded:

> We were all afraid of the Coastwatcher who was like the government man, and the headman. Their orders were the law and if you didn't obey, they put you over a drum and gave you 12 or so whips … you know that time, the word of the government was the last word. We were afraid, not like now when plenty of people are clever [educated] (WPA 1988: 1).

Caleb Alu, another veteran of the war, recalled his service under coastwatcher Josselyn: 'Josselyn was a rough man … everybody was afraid of him. Only small things and he would whip you' (ibid.: 7). Alfred Bisili also described corporal punishment as used by Kennedy on scouts who were slow in dispatching reports to the coastwatching station at Seghe. All information gathered by scouts on Japanese troops needed to reach the responsible coastwatcher within 24 hours. Delays in reporting were not tolerated by Kennedy, who usually investigated the causes of interruption. Bisili (1988: 80) stated 'those guilty of the delay received very severe beatings with *loia* [lawyer] cane. For many who experienced these beatings they will still be fresh in their minds'.

District Officer Donald Kennedy, a New Zealander, was a well-known coastwatcher in the Solomons. His colonial service began in Fiji where he was appointed to teach at the Suva Grammar School in 1921. A year later, Kennedy became the headmaster at the Banaban School in Gilbert and Ellice Islands,[6] also establishing a school at Vaitupu for Ellice Islanders. Despite his success, he was transferred to Tarawa as acting headmaster due to accusations of violence, womanising, alcoholism and a stormy relationship with his superiors. In 1932, he returned to Ellice Islands as acting administrative officer and later lands commissioner. But his difficult

---

6   Formerly Kiribati and Tuvalu, respectively.

attitude again got in the way and he was removed after complaints from colonial colleagues and a petition from islanders. He was then posted to the British Solomon Islands where he worked as a district officer and became actively involved in Allied war efforts in the protectorate (Laracy 2013: 211–14).

His notorious reputation and violent behaviour became both a blessing and a curse to islanders who served under his authority in the British Solomon Islands Protectorate. His methods of punishment included lashes ordered by him and often carried out by other scouts. His violence towards indigenous people inevitably shaped social relationships. Although Bill Bennett compliments Kennedy's heavy-handedness as appropriate to his leadership responsibilities during the war, no other scouts who served in his force expressed this view. Most documented recollections repeatedly express the harshness of Kennedy's disciplinary actions. Kitchener Ada, who served as a scout under Kennedy, recalled:

> Kennedy whipped me. We used to have stations to watch. One night I was assigned to No. 3 station. An airplane came, but I had a sore on the leg and so I just lay down on a log and slept. So they never had any report from me that night, because I was asleep (laughs). So I went to court. Kennedy asked what I would have done if the enemy had come — I said, we're here to fight, so I would have fought. But he said I broke the military order, so he said I could choose three whips or one-pound fine. So I thought hard about that. One pound was about a month's pay, but three whips was for only a second or two, not every day. So I said, 'Master, I think I'll take the whip' (laughs). Pinenunu, a Gela man, did the whipping. He was Kennedy's cook. I was cross after that and didn't want to work. There was plenty of us got whipped. It wasn't always big things that got you in trouble. People would report others for small things. I wondered, couldn't they just forget these things? And many times it was our chiefs who were reporting us for small things we did. Later we thought, we could have just shot them. And maybe in old times, we could just have eaten them (WPA 1988: 30).

While Ada's punishment might have been reasonable for his offence, Kennedy's disciplinary actions induced a sense of 'loyalty' in the local population based on the fear of being lashed or having a month's worth of wages denied. Scout Jim Bennett, the brother of Bill Bennett, described Kennedy as a 'fright-inspiring man' who gave orders and expected the response 'yes sir or no sir' (WPA 1988: 106). In his oral recollection, Daniel Gua also mentioned the brutality of Kennedy's disciplinary actions:

'even though we were far away from him [Kennedy], we felt he was the boss because anybody could report you and you'd get into trouble' (WPA 1988: 94). Beyond compelling 'loyalty', this strict standard of discipline created a platform advantageously exploited by indigenous people to avenge themselves against each other on the slightest issue of personal conflict or discontent within society. It left an impact on social relationships among individuals, as expressed by Ada and Gua's recollections.[7]

Mike Butcher, who has thoroughly researched the life of Donald Kennedy in the Pacific, acknowledged that Kennedy had personal shortcomings that affected his relationships with islanders (Butcher 2012: 53–76, 131–84). Among islanders who worked for him or lived under his authority, Kennedy was a character who commanded respect and did not tolerate mistakes. The fear of his authority and dislike of his conduct was a common theme in postwar reminiscences among local veterans.

One story that has created significant discussion in the public sphere is the confession of Bill Bennett, who was second-in-command to Kennedy during the war. Bennett claimed to have shot Kennedy in the leg during a confrontation with a Japanese whaleboat on Marovo lagoon, Western Solomons (Crowe 1987). The incident, known as the 'Battle of Marovo', was long known to have left Kennedy with an injured leg (COI 1946: 49–53; Horton 1970: 209–211; Lord 1977: 206–8). Bennett said he intentionally shot Kennedy in revenge for an incident that resulted in Kennedy ordering one of his boys to lash Bennett with *loia* [lawyer] cane while he was forced to lie across a 44-gallon fuel drum. Bennett described how he was ordered by Kennedy to find him a local woman to satisfy his sexual desires. Bennett set out looking, but returned empty handed. This made Kennedy furious so he ordered that Bennett be punished for his failure (Crowe 1987). Butcher proposed that Bennett's shooting might not have been intentional but triggered by anxiety and fear during the confrontation with the enemy, and that Bennett, who was under the influence of alcohol at the time of Crowe's interview, might have made up the story for a specifically 'truth seeking audience' (Butcher 2012: 64). But Bennett's confession and the oral testimonies of other scouts who served under Kennedy during the war is intriguing. Taken together, these

---

7   Bennett also expressed similar sentiments of discontent concerning Kennedy's punishments when interviewed by Peter Crowe (1987). See also Bennett (1988).

accounts depict the extent to which coercion and the threat of punishment contributed to the control maintained by the colonial authorities over the indigenous population.[8]

For islanders like native medical practitioner George Bogese, infliction of penalties by colonial authorities bore even harsher consequences than physical punishment. A native of Isabel Island, Bogese was the first Solomon Islander to be sent by the colonial administration to pursue medical studies in Fiji. Unlike other islanders' heroic stories of the war, Bogese came to be regarded as a 'traitor' to the coastwatching network. Like other scouts, Bogese did not have a functional relationship with Donald Kennedy. Assigning Bogese to Savo Island before the war, Kennedy instructed the headman on Savo to kill Bogese if he misbehaved and warned Bogese to 'be very careful, or you will be shot, or whipped, the same as the others' (Laracy 2013: 236).[9] On 4 May 1942, during the initial landing of Japanese troops on Tulagi, the Japanese destroyer *Kitsutsuki* was sunk and the next day two survivors were found ashore on Savo. Bogese offered medical treatment to the Japanese sailors. However, he was not the only one who assisted in their care: coastwatcher Leif Shroeder and missionary Desmond Scanlon both offered food and clothing to the sailors. Four days later, a Japanese barge landed at Savo, guided by a Savo native who identified Bogese. The Japanese threatened Bogese and forced him to accompany them to Tulagi where he assisted in the translation of Japanese notices into local vernaculars. As Bogese later attested, he 'was frightened to disobey' the Japanese (Laracy 2013: 231). From this point on, Bogese had an enemy on both sides: Kennedy and the colonial administration on one hand and the Japanese on the other.

Bogese had not seen his family since his posting to Savo, so when ordered to Rabaul to meet with the Japanese chief medical officer, Bogese asked if he could visit his family. Escorted by 50 Japanese soldiers, Bogese travelled to Isabel to bring his family to Tulagi. On the return journey, the Japanese encountered and sank Kennedy's vessel the *Wai-ai* at Mahaga in Isabel. Bogese remained under the jurisdiction of the Japanese until he was 'captured' by the Allies in early August 1942. At the persuasion of the British administration, he was interned in Australia with his family until October 1945 (Bogese n.d.). Upon his return to the protectorate, Bogese

---

8 The story of Bill Bennett shooting Donald Kennedy, and Butcher's interpretation, are also discussed in White (2015: 216) and Laracy (2013).
9 See also Laracy (1991: 59–75).

was tried on five counts of collaboration with the Japanese. Four charges were dismissed but he was convicted of the fifth, which stated that he 'did voluntarily join himself with the enemy Japanese between 1 May and 8 August 1942' (Laracy 2013: 238; see also Bennett 1988: 144–5). Bogese was sentenced to four years' imprisonment and was released in 1949.

Bogese's story exemplifies the extent of penalties an islander could incur for any form of interaction with Japanese troops perceived by British colonial officers as collaboration. Bogese's conviction was a judgement by the colonial administration against his character and lack of 'loyalty', with a biased consideration of the threats levelled at him by the Japanese to ensure he cooperated with their orders. It can be argued that the severity of Bogese's punishment was a demonstration by the colonial administration aimed at reasserting its prewar authority and control over the local population.

Curiosity and adventure

World War II was extraordinarily memorable for Solomon Islanders, in both the scale and the manner in which it was fought. War was not a new concept for Solomon Islands cultures, but it was previously fought on a far smaller scale between tribal groups. Such skirmishes were usually a form of revenge or demonstration of power between groups within or between islands. The way wars were fought was always of an unsettling nature among the tribal parties concerned and limited in setting. World War II, on the other hand, operated on a global scale that was beyond the understanding of islanders. The equipment used, the materials shipped in and the armed forces themselves were massive on both the Allied and Japanese sides. The nature of the fighting and why it came to their islands was not understood by islanders, and was questioned repeatedly. Indeed, islanders were in a state of confusion over the war, and so relied heavily on information and instructions from their head men, missionaries and district officers. The massive scale of the war and subsequent events also sparked curiosity and provided opportunities for adventure among young men. And although young islanders of this generation generally preferred the Allied forces over the Japanese, it was also partly the nature of their encounters with both sides that motivated them to choose one over the other.

3. WHY SUPPORT THE ALLIES?

As news of Japan's occupation of Tulagi spread through the protectorate, a powerful sense of curiosity and thirst for adventure emerged among young men all over the British Solomon Islands Protectorate. These impulses fed the influx of younger men signing on for scouting and labour during the war. At the end of the Solomon Islands Campaign, more than 800 men were enlisted in the British Solomon Islands Defence Force and records indicate a labour strength of over 3,700 recruits by July 1944 (Solomon Islands National Archives 1945). Scout Alfred Alasasa Bisili recalled the landing of Japanese troops at Munda in November 1942:

> It was very late in the afternoon, about 5 pm or so. We saw five Japanese battleships anchored outside Munda Bar. At about seven in the evening the soldiers came ashore. The five battleships then left. Where to, no one knew. But most probably to the Shortlands or to Rabaul in Papua New Guinea. The following day being very curious about the landing of the Japs, I, Solomon Hitu, and Nebot Kiada decided to go and investigate (Bisili 1988: 80–1).

Bisili's account of his and his friends' encounter with Japanese troops reveals the level of curiosity and the urge 'to go and investigate' prevalant among young islanders, despite the possible dangers. Similar sentiments led Biuku Gasa to join the scouting network. In his recollection, he stated: 'I was interested to become a scout from the time I first saw the planes come around Munda. I wanted to see the war and how people fought' (Gasa and Kumana 1988: 85).

In his book *Island Administration in the South West Pacific*, Cyril Belshaw, acting district officer in Gela in 1944–45 (who for a time produced a typewritten newspaper in the local vernacular), recorded some experiences of indigenous people of the area during the war. In an appendix to his book, he included translated narrations titled 'Native attitudes during the war'. Belshaw indicated that the texts were compiled and translated into English by his local clerk. In the transcribed narrations, an anonymous man of the Gela detachment of the Solomon Islands Labour Corps, working on Guadalcanal, described his curiosity in a more detailed way, including what he saw, his amazement at the machinery used by the military and the different groups of people he encountered. He described the air force, the ground forces, the marines and even medics in great detail as he understood them:

While I was at my home I heard the news all about Guadalcanal its all over my island for the people and everything. I was hoping to get there and see what its all about whether its true or not. Now I'm come and saw what's all about and its true all the news I heard. These I saw on the 16.1.44 and I was surprise to see them: (i) plenty of people, (ii) the ships on the sea, (iii) the airplanes, (iv) the launches, (v) the ships it goes in sea and in land, (vi) all sorts of launches, (vii) all sorts of different languages, (viii) all sorts of men, white and brown and black. Every tribes are in here (1) Americans, (2) Solomon Islander — these are plenty in here, (3) New Zealanders, (4) Australians, (5) Hawaiians, (6) Fijians, (7) Englanders. Although call them all Englanders because words gathered them together. These are all kinds of work they entered in (1) marines, (2) army, (3) navy, (4) air force, (5) labour, (6) doctor. Their business: the marines are to fight on land and occupies every parts of our islands. The navy are they fighting on board just exactly the same as the marines. Airmen are fighting in the air by the planes. The army are to take over the place and use it for war. The doctor to take care for the wounded and sick patients. Where they camp? I could not tell lies but I don't know where and where they all stayed in here at Guadalcanal. There are make me so surprise, for the looking at all sorts of things. I did not heard any news from my fathers and grandfathers could tell me the things like these before and this is my first time I saw it. These makes me so surprise (1) the airplanes (2) ships (3) motor cars (4) bombs (5) truck car (6) the ships it goes on sea as in land (7) all kinds of food (8) plenty of people (9) all kinds of play (10) the garden are so larger the length are 150 acre also the width (11) there all the American works (12) they win the fight (13) their great love of our Allied for they gave up their lives and they died for us (Belshaw 1950: 143–4).

These expressions of an islander demonstrate the extent to which the war shaped islanders' understanding of modern warfare and technology. It also suggests two major issues for understanding local involvement in the war. First, it depicts the extent to which curiosity drove able-bodied men from their villages to places where they could get a glimpse of military activities, or simply to ascertain that what they had heard, perhaps from other members of their communities, were not just rumours. Second, islanders were amazed and overwhelmed by what they saw. The machines, categories of military forces, groups of people, their nationalities and the specific tasks performed by each group were sources of apparent fascination to islanders who had never seen anything like this before or even heard talk of such things from their elders.

The material and military superiority of the American forces impressed islanders at every level, and would have provided substantial rationale for indigenous allegiance to Allied forces during the war if there had been no other reason for such loyalty. John Kari from Rendova in Western Province was one of the educated elite of his society. When recounting his wartime experiences, Kari compared the military strength of American and Japanese troops and made statements similar to those of the anonymous islander from Gela quoted above, opining that the Japanese were not a force to reckon with and that the Americans had superior artillery and possessed military equipment that the Japanese lacked (Kari and Langabaea 1988: 98–9).[10] Likewise, Sergeant Andrew Langabaea began his narrative memories of the war by commenting on the military superiority of the United States as he observed it. He recalled the amazement of islanders when Americans landed on Guadalcanal on 7 August 1942: 'you could have walked on ships from Marau to Tulagi the morning they came to start the landings. Barges, warships, cruisers, battleships … we just saw for the first time the way white men fight' (ibid.: 99).[11] Although Langabaea's statement is factually exaggerated, it again indicates the overwhelming impact the war had on islanders' understandings. George Maelalo, who had frontline experience with the Americans to as far as Bougainville, noted that the United States Marines were well trained for battle, but also that Japanese troops were not a force to underestimate — they were very skilful in jungle fighting and 'when you look at the two kinds of soldiers side-by-side there was a definite difference between them in the way they looked and fought. The Japanese were small but you can tell they were well trained' (Maelalo 1988: 189).

Communications

In the British Solomon Islands, there were over 80 native languages spoken by indigenous peoples. This did not make communication simple for any foreigner, especially Japanese soldiers who did not speak Pidgin or English (Wurm and Hattori 1981–83). Pidgin was the evolving lingua franca used by the British administration and expatriate community in

---

10 See also oral recollection of Daniel Rereqeto in WPA (1988: 18). Daniel was not formally enlisted in the scouting network but described his amazement at America's military and material strength. His description noted Americans as 'powerful' in their infrastructure construction at Barakoma and Lambulambu.
11 See also oral recollection of Robert Bula in WPA (1988: 95–104).

the protectorate. However, it was used and understood by only a small fraction of the population, mainly those who worked on plantations and in the public service. Others who obtained some formal Western education, either overseas in Fiji or at local schools run by missionaries, were able to speak and understand English. Even though Pidgin and English were used by a minority of the native population, this still placed Allied troops in an advantageous position over Japanese troops during the war.

The difficulty encountered by islanders in communicating with Japanese troops inhibited understanding between the two parties. Sign language was used, but its effectiveness was minimal. Scout Alfred Bisili confirmed that communication with Japanese soldiers was indeed challenging. When recalling his first encounter with Japanese soldiers, he stated, 'we couldn't understand what they were saying to us … we used hand sign language before we managed to get what they wanted' (Bisili 1988: 81). George Maelalo also highlighted the barrier of language, saying 'if he [Japanese] were an Englishman I could talk to him … but, my word, I could not speak Japanese' (Maelalo 1988: 188).

The hurdle of language was not disregarded by Japanese military officials when they occupied the Solomons. In an attempt to disseminate a declaration of their occupation of Solomon Islands, native medical practitioner George Bogese was coerced by the Japanese to translate into local languages two notices issued by the commander of the imperial navy (as mentioned earlier in the chapter under 'Infliction of penalties'). However, little was accomplished in the attempt to communicate to islanders behaviour expected by Japanese troops, and attempts at spreading any form of propaganda against Allied nations failed.

Employment and increases in wages

The Solomons Campaign saw an increase in wages for indigenous services provided to Allied troops and, as a result, demand for jobs also increased among the local population. Before the war, indigenous labour was required mainly for plantation work. Islanders were recruited for a period of one to three years for wages of one pound per month. During the global economic depression of the 1930s, the price for copra dropped drastically,[12] resulting in the halving of wages to 10 shillings per month.

---

12 Copra is the dried kernel from a coconut, used for its oil. It was the main export commodity of the British Solomon Islands Protectorate before the war.

As war proceeded in the protectorate, the demand for labour in military service became urgent and resulted in a rise in wages to attract labourers. Local wages rebounded from 10 shillings back to one pound per month, and in some cases labourers were able to earn up to 14 pounds in a month (Figure 15) (Belshaw 1950: 69). The effects of the increase in local wages will be discussed in detail in the next chapter; however, there was an immediate influx of labourers from all over the islands seeking paid employment from Allied forces.

Figure 15: Workers line up to receive weekly wages of five shillings (80 cents) from Australian Major J.V. Mather, Guadalcanal, 28 January 1943. Note the military cameraman at work
Source: United States Marine Corps (photo 52765), United States National Archives.

The Japanese, on the other hand, attempted to recruit islanders for labour without paid wages. In two documents distributed to villages by Japanese officials, there is no indication of any form of wages for local labour, but rather sets of orders pertaining to the confiscation of all properties in the protectorate, as well as the expected moral conduct and assurance of security to those who abided by the laws of Japan (including missionaries and Europeans).¹³ Whatever the Japanese Empire aimed to achieve in the Solomons, it did not use wages as a means to achieve it, relying instead on force or the threat of force by Japanese soldiers.

Britain — 'our government'

The colonial history of Great Britain in Solomon Islands was another motivating factor for islanders' allegiance to the Allied nations during the campaign. First, there was a sense of political affiliation among the local population towards Britain as their government. Second, there were comparisons made by islanders on military strength and different categories and attitudes of peoples they encountered during the war. Japan was constrained by circumstances that seemed less favourable to the local population.

British Solomon Islands Protectorate was an ethnically diverse group of islands. When Britain declared a protectorate in 1893, a government administration was established that became a unifying medium for the cultural and linguistic diversity of the island group. This is not to say that traditional affiliations of individual ethnic groups ceased to exist, but several decades of colonialism encouraged a mentality of identification with Britain as the local government during the war. Shortly after the Japanese advancement into Solomon Islands in early 1942, islanders began to perceive that their islands were being occupied by Japanese armies because of the colonial government's alliance with the United States. The Japanese were viewed as an enemy attacking the government, not simply a political opponent with whom they might affiliate. Although the nature of the war was barely understood by the indigenous population, the notion of protecting its government from strange enemies became a motive for participation. There emerged a unified, but not altogether voluntary, sense of patriotism among islanders. As Andrew Langabaea, a sergeant of the Solomon Islands Defence Force who served with Martin Clemens during the war expressed it, 'you might think I was a volunteer to do all this fighting business, but at that time, they [district officers] said there weren't enough men so I must stay. So I did' (Kari and Langabaea 1988: 102). Loyd Gina, who later became a politician in the Solomon Islands

---

13   The Catholic Archdiocese of Honiara, reference box 'War', cited in Laracy and White (1988: 145–6).

Government, explained that the nature of Solomon Islands' involvement in the war was determined by its status as a British territory. As a result of their colonial status, he noted that islanders were obliged to offer their allegiance to Allied forces during the war (Crowe 1987).

The islanders' understanding of the outside world was limited, and Japan was not known as a country or even heard of prior to the war. Even if the word 'Japan' did ring a bell in people's minds, it was only through knowledge of individual Japanese who had been in the protectorate before the war (Clemens 1998: 31). The United States, too, was probably never heard of by the majority of the indigenous population. Oral recollections reveal how little knowledge islanders had of the world beyond their shores. George Maelalo recalled that while he and a few others had seen American sailors before the war, most people had no knowledge of America or how to distinguish an American from other Europeans (Maelalo 1988: 180). However, the alliance of the United States with Britain created a foundation for islander acceptance of American servicemen as friends in indigenous communities during the war.

Comparisons of attitudes

Limited knowledge of the outside world did not limit the ability of islanders to compare the attitudes of the Japanese and Americans they encountered during the war. The arrival of Japanese and American troops in 1942 meant the introduction of additional sets of cultures into the diversity that already existed in the protectorate. Because the United States was an ally of Britain and had a similar language and culture, it was easily acceptable to local societies. Japanese troops were blinkered by a strong sense of cultural imperialism and failed to take into account the norms and customs that governed the occupied societies. As a result, societal norms and local customs were trampled upon by Japanese troops. The Imperial Army occupied churches as barracks and removed any ornaments of value to send back to Japan. Whatever their needs were, they felt that they could be obtained from villagers at gunpoint, and all able-bodied males were forced to labour for no wages with the threat of extermination of entire villages upon refusal to work for the Japanese Empire (COI 1946: 20).

In recalling experiences of the war on different occasions, local veterans never ceased to comment on the attitude of Japanese troops towards their property, churches and customs. One scout recalled: 'You know, before we scouts were even set up in Vonavona, the Japanese went inside the lagoon. They went into the church at Madou and ate, and shit in there too' (Kari and Langabaea 1988: 98). Leslie Miki, a scout of Geoffrey Kuper, recalled a Japanese fighter plane that made an emergency landing at a village in Kia, Isabel Island. Miki recalled that the plane was out of fuel and the pilots stayed at the village until another plane was sent to their rescue. While the pilots were in the village, Miki described that 'they used the church at Kia like it was their house for sleeping. They just "borrowed" any pineapples or oranges in the Kia area and brought them back to eat. They didn't see the church as a house for worship' (Zaku et al. 1988: 156). But the Americans were different: they respected indigenous property and mainly shared the same Christian faith. Andrew Langabaea recalled 'the Americans, no matter how rough things would become, would always go to church' (Kari and Langabaea 1988: 103). There was an expectation among local peoples that foreigners (Japanese troops and Allied troops) be aware of religious sites, in this case churches, and their importance to society. Such perceptions informed islanders' comparative perspectives and help to explain their support of the Allied forces.

Cyril Belshaw's recorded experiences of Gela people during the war repeatedly echoed local resentment towards Japanese behaviour as they encountered it. Another anonymous islander relates:

> This is about the Japanese. They went to all the villages and they stole the following foods: bananas, pineapples, pigs, fowls, etc. they did these when they stayed at Tulagi, Makambo, Gavutu, Tanambogo and Halavo. Then they killed and died before they finished spoil and stolen all our things in the whole Gela. Those are the unkindly tribes in the world for they treat us so badly. When the Americans attacked them … some escaped to Gela's jungle and they stayed there and start to get hungry and some of them died in cause of hunger, and some went to the beach and get raw coconuts and crabs clams and some other shells and they went to the bush and stole yams, pannas in our gardens to eat with shell (Belshaw 1950: 142).

Sao, a scout from Isabel, developed a different perspective from his encounters with Japanese soldiers. His interaction with the Japanese occurred when he and his fellow scout rescued and returned Japanese soldiers to their military base at Suavana on Isabel Island. Enlightened by this close encounter, Sao said:

the Japanese were good people too. They didn't make all sorts of trouble. They were just young men. Some weren't even shaving yet, just really young men. If those things happened with some Americans we might have died. Sometimes we just paddled very near them, actually went and scouted right in front of their eyes. When we or Mostyn went they would say, 'You all don't come near here. If the Americans come and bomb you might get hit.' That's what they told us. But if it had been like that with the Americans, it would have been all over. They would have shot us. Because if they saw us nearby like that, they would shoot. But not the Japanese. They just gave instructions, 'you all don't ever come near, otherwise when the American planes come and bomb they might miss the guns and get you'. That's just how it was (Zaku et al. 1988: 166–7).

Despite this positive opinion of the Japanese soldiers, Sao indicated his allegiance to the Allies as a scout. His alternative perception of Japanese soldiers is an example of a more humanitarian viewpoint, and was not unique. Other oral testimonies have also shed light on this aspect of islander–military relations, which will be discussed in the next chapter.[14]

Conclusion

I have shown in this chapter the different motivations that influenced the involvement of islanders in the war and local attitudes towards both Allied and Japanese troops. There were feelings of obligation that can be understood by examining the structure of the society and the colonial experience. The local societal hierarchy had been integrated into the British administration of indigenous affairs, and traditional leaders were either appointed or empowered by the administration. Feelings of obligation were also evoked by the principles of Christianity and the good relationships that were established between missionaries and islanders. Beyond this, propaganda spread by district officers throughout the islands also played a part in moulding islander attitudes towards Japanese troops. Also, penalties and punishment were imposed on islanders by coastwatchers, compelling cooperation with the Allies.

Beyond these 'push' factors, there was a strong sense of curiosity and lust for adventure among young male islanders, drawn by fascination with large-scale military developments and equipment, which became

---

14 See also oral recollections of Danial Gua (pp. 87–94) and John and Joyce Wheatley Kevisi (pp. 67–70) in WPA (1988).

a 'pull' factor towards involvement in the war. Meanwhile, the Allies' demand for local labour and the rise in local wages saw a large number of islanders enlist in the campaign. Another factor was the difficulty of communication with Japanese troops. Islanders found communicating with Japanese soldiers challenging, and this challenge became an advantage to Allied troops. Finally, since islanders had become familiar with British administration, invasion by a foreign power triggered a sense of patriotism and identification with the Allies. Islanders not only had the ability to compare attitudes and categorise different groups of peoples during the war, they could also assess the comparative strength of men and arms and the progress of the war. This ability enabled them to wisely choose to remain on the Allied side.

4
Impacts of the War

The Solomon Islands Campaign was more than a significant milestone in the history of the British Solomon Islands Protectorate and its people. Rapid change affected islanders' outlook and their surrounding environment during and after the war. These changes set the stage for the struggle towards Solomon Islands independence from Britain in 1978. Today, many of these changes are still visible in the physical and human landscapes of the country. This chapter will explore the impacts and effects of the Pacific War on Solomon Islands and its people. The first section will deal with the immediate impacts of war, while the second section discusses political change, social change and economic development in the postwar period.

Immediate effects of the war

The arrival of the Pacific War in Solomon Islands had a dramatic impact on all aspects of indigenous social life. Islanders' world view and understanding of racial relationships developed considerably, through encounters with military troops of both the Allied and Japanese sides. Perceptions and attitudes towards the British administration took a new turn during the war as islanders interacted with members of the United States military forces. For the first time since Britain established a protectorate over Solomon Islands, individual islanders were able to interact on a new level with white men: sharing cigarettes, eating together and performing the same tasks as the white soldiers. This set new standards for islanders, and at the same time provided both reason and opportunity for expressing resentment towards their white colonial masters and the British administration. An example of such feelings can be found in the words of scout John Kari of Western District:

> it seemed before the war that the Europeans who were around don't really like black people around them. They could never sit down and just story, or eat. They only talked to their own kind. But when the Americans came, they really went inside the local people; it was the first time for us to see this. Also, the British wouldn't come ashore through the water. A man would carry them. I remember an American saw one of the Solomon Islanders carrying Mr Horton. He said, 'what, is he sick or lame? Is he taking him to the hospital?' and they didn't like to see the Americans give us smokes. We would always hide from the government men to get smokes, and the Americans would ask what the problem was. Was it wrong for us to smoke? The government would say we had to work, but the Americans would turn around and say, 'the machines do the work, not the hands' (Gasa and Kumana 1988: 98–9).

Two significant issues are expressed by Kari. First, there was only limited social interaction between indigenous people and whites prior to the war. The relationship that islanders had with the prewar white community of the British protectorate was a 'master–boy' relationship. Islanders always regarded white government officials, traders and missionaries as 'masters' and powerful agents in their societies. Meanwhile, many whites considered the 'native' a primitive savage. Islanders were not seen as racially equal to 'white men', and day-to-day social interaction between the parties was discouraged. The extremes of this racial imbalance can be seen in a 1922 complaint to the High Commissioner for the South West Pacific by the chairman of Levers Pacific Plantations Ltd, on the alleged mistreatment of islanders by three Australian overseers who were transported to Fiji to face trial for the murder of a Malaitan labourer. Joseph Meek, the chairman for Levers, wrote to the high commissioner in defence of the overseers, stating:

> We submit for the consideration of the government that when a white man is arrested in the Solomon Islands, and when he has to be conveyed from the Solomon Islands to Fiji that there should be white quarters with the white man's accommodation, and that the white race should not have their dignity lowered by being put into a hold with the ordinary 'Boys'. In fact, only by doing this can one preserve the dignity, not merely of the white man, but of the white Government. It does not seem to have been practised in this case, and these men seem to have just reason for complaint (Meek to High Commissioner, 22 June 1922, WPHC 4, 1862/22, Western Pacific Archives).

Such feelings as expressed by Meek depict the racism in the British protectorate before the war, and its connections to colonial rule. These white racial sentiments were not ignored by islanders. Jonathan Fifi'i, a houseboy for Sister Cleaver, an Australian nurse in Tulagi before the war, described his experience of racial segregation in the colonial headquarters: 'Tulagi was a strange place then … the white people all segregated up on the hill, with their hotel and their club; and the Chinese down in Chinatown … we Solomon Islanders were at the very bottom of the heap' (Fifi'i 1989: 34). Fifi'i also recalled his encounter with S.G. Masterman, the inspector of 'Native Labour' for the protectorate, to exemplify the extent of racism at Tulagi. Fifi'i, on his way to buy bread, rode past Masterman on his bicycle. Masterman yelled out to Fifi'i to stop and get off his bicycle. In doing so, Masterman lectured Fifi'i that 'when you see a white man, you can't go past him on your bicycle. You get off and stand at attention until he goes past … because white people are the rulers here. You natives are nothing. If you see a white man, you have to give him proper respect' (ibid.: 35). The treatment of islanders as an inferior group did not go unrecognised by the celebrated Anglican missionary, Charles Fox, who stated that the islanders felt:

> very much being treated as inferiors. The colour feeling is real. The test of colour feelings is whether a man will eat with another or not. That is the Melanesia test. No Government official or trader will allow Melanesians to eat with him or even drink a cup of tea with him, for the sake of British prestige. But that is the Melanesian test (Hilliard 1978: 272).

There were exceptions in the case of some missionaries whose intentions were to spread Christianity to islanders. For this purpose, missionaries had a daily social interface with indigenous peoples and their affairs. However, missionaries' collaboration with islanders did not erase racial demarcations. Fifi'i deduced that 'the Christianity we were given taught us to be peaceful and obedient, like well-behaved children — not equal to white people' (Fifi'i 1989: 41). Any Europeans who ventured over the racial line were accused of 'going native'. Such was the case of the Methodist missionary Reverend J.F. Goldie, who was among the first team of missionaries of the Methodist Mission Society of Australia who went to Solomon Islands in 1902. Their pioneering effort to Christianise Solomon Islands was highly successful and islanders thought so highly of Goldie that he became their voice in liaising with government administrators, planters and traders, who demanded land at low cost or sought to alienate it for plantation purposes. Goldie's position as a missionary ensured that islanders' welfare was prioritised. However, he was often accused of 'interfering' with matters and even of 'going native' by having a personal interest in islanders' affairs (Luxton 1955: 117–18). Because of the missionaries' collaborative efforts with indigenous peoples, it is important to note that when islanders mentioned 'Europeans' they were mainly referring to white planters, traders and some of the British administrative officers. Solomon Islander academic Tarcisius Kabutaulaka wrote, 'although the District Officer was frequently friendly towards Solomon Islanders, he treated them as inferior because he did not want to identify himself with them' (Kabutaulaka 1990: 43). Hence, it is evident that the social environment in the protectorate during the prewar period was divided by a racial line of 'white' superiority over the inferior 'black race' of which the islanders were a part.

The second point expressed by Kari was that the war provided an avenue for interracial interaction in marked contrast to indigenous experiences before 1942. Islanders were able to mingle with people of 'white' origin for the first time and became able to differentiate white people according to their nationalities. This ability saw a marked bias develop in favour of American troops over British colonial administrators. The statement by John Kari that Americans 'really went inside the local people' is an expression of the extent to which indigenous perceptions of interracial relationships with American troops were shaped by the war. Scout Andrew Langabaea made a statement similar to Kari's, recalling 'the Americans would say the skin was different, but the life and blood was one kind … before you always had to say, "yes, sir" and "no, sir" but not with the Americans. Any man was just "Joe" ' (Gasa and Kumana 1988: 103). George Maelalo, who had frontline experience with the fighting forces, had an even more specific outlook on Allied soldiers according to their nationalities:

> The Joes were a different kind of people when they were in the bush. They did not care about anything. If they wanted to do something, they went ahead and did it. There was one thing that I noticed about the American soldiers. They did not have much respect for their officers. Rarely had I seen a soldier respond promptly to an officer by saying 'here, sir'. After the officer had left, the soldier would say, 'one of these days I will put a bullet in your head'. They were not like Australian soldiers. Australian soldiers thought very highly of their officers. The soldiers obeyed their officers very much (Maelalo 1988: 185).

These expressions indicate the superiority of the colonial administration over islanders before 1942, and islanders' realisation of opportunities for new cross-cultural relations emerging from the war. This development can be seen from the vocabulary of formal addresses to British officers as compared to American soldiers. The words 'Sir' and 'Master' were the only terms used to address men of European heritage before the war. When the Americans entered the war, 'Joe' became the common address for white American soldiers. As Maelalo observes, the word 'Sir' was not accustomed usage for American soldiers. Like other islanders, Maelalo began to question the genuineness of the prestige claimed by colonial officers.

Not only did the war reshape islanders' world views, it also laid a foundation for political education. The opportunity to interact with white American soldiers set an educational milestone for indigenous peoples, who began to challenge colonial dominance over them. This does not suggest that islanders were unaware of issues of racism in the protectorate prior to the Solomon Islands Campaign. In fact, expressions of dissatisfaction had occurred before the war and, as Hugh Laracy has argued, many islanders' dislike of the colonial regime was evident well before the war. Resentment had been demonstrated through conflicts with planters and district officers. An example was the killing of district officer William Bell on east Malaita in 1927. His murder occurred as a result of his attempt to collect head tax and confiscate rifles from islanders (Laracy 1983: 12). These rifles were either obtained from traders or purchased by those who had been to Queensland as labourers. Although confiscating rifles from islanders could be seen as an appropriate measure by the administration to put an end to tribal conflict throughout the protectorate, it did not seem right to the islanders who owned the rifles. The possession of a rifle was a source of power among tribal groups, and confiscating one would put the tribe at risk of attacks from its enemies. After the murder of Bell, massive retaliation was carried out by the government, resulting in the deaths of hundreds of civilian islanders and the destruction of houses, gardens and villages. In late June 1928, those who were convicted of Bell's murder were hanged (ibid.: 8).

This massive reprisal demonstrated the administration's ability to control the population, but islander discontent with the British administration continued to grow. As Laracy argued:

there is no reason to suppose that Solomon Islanders have ever been less conscious of their worth than have any other people … the historical record clearly attests to their abundant readiness to defend both themselves and that which they considered to be theirs (ibid.: 7; see also Akin 2013).

A sense of admiration became evident among islanders as they saw black American soldiers enjoying equal opportunities in the battlefield with white GIs. The observation that black GIs wore the same clothes, slept under the same tents and had the same rations as white soldiers sparked inquisitiveness and captivated the imagination of islanders. Jonathan Fifi'i, a sergeant of the Solomon Islands Labour Corps and district head chief of the Maasina Rule, a nationalist sociopolitical movement that emerged after the war, recalled:

> We did the same kind of work as the Americans and the British, but we weren't allowed to wear the same kinds of uniforms. We wore lavalavas, yardage. It was forbidden for us to wear trousers or shirts. We sergeants were given a piece of khaki that had three stripes painted on it. They tied strings onto the cloth, and each of us were to tie the cloth onto our arms. The white officers all wore their stripes sewn onto their shirts, but all we got were those pieces of khaki. I was ashamed to wear it like that, so I would just carry it around in my hand (Fifi'i 1991: 41).

Fifi'i's statement demonstrates that Solomon Islanders were not unaware of the racial allusions of colonial officers. When questioned about whether Americans gave uniforms to islanders, Gafu, a member of the labour corps replied, 'No, we only wore *lavalavas* [sarongs] because we were just labourers. The black Americans, however, wore uniforms. It was our ordinary clothing that made it easy for the Americans to identify us' (Ngwadili and Gafu 1988: 209). It might be that islanders perceived themselves as equals to black GIs but perceived white soldiers as superior. If so, this observation will have contributed to islanders' quest to improve their status relative to their white colonial 'masters'.

Indigenous people enjoyed the food and friendship shared with generous American soldiers. David Gegeo stated this gave rise to a 'mythic schema' of the abundant wealth and racial equality of Americans (Gegeo 1991: 30). Islander impressions of United States society, of course, did not correspond with the racial situation that actually existed in America. Whether islanders were aware of racial discrimination that existed among American soldiers was not evident in their oral recollections. What is evident was the equal treatment they experienced at the hands of both black and white American soldiers. Gafu recalled 'they [Americans] outnumbered us but there was not a feeling of white versus black among us. We all stay together as if we were of one race' (Ngwadili and Gafu 1988: 209–10). However, Arnon Ngwadili, the caretaker of Resident Commissioner William Marchant, described how the 'Black Joes' would often come to the residence to inquire about who owned the house or who lived in the house. Ngwadili stated 'the white Americans are alright'. He recalled that sometimes he was afraid of the coloured Americans because of their physical build. But realising his responsibility as caretaker, he often refused their attempt to enter the commissioner's house (ibid.: 205). To islanders, close association with white soldiers changed their understandings of the racial relationships to which they were accustomed under the British administration. Scout Essau Hiele commented that war left a positive imprint because 'people's minds are open, eyes were open, [and] brains were open, to outside things. People no longer find it difficult to understand new things' (WPA 1988: 21).

This transformation of views was not unique to Solomon Islands. In neighbouring Papua New Guinea, similar perceptions of prewar interracial relationships prevailed among indigenous people. Like the experiences of Solomon Islanders, the war also brought experiences in contrast to the prewar white master/black servant relationship for indigenous people in Papua New Guinea. John Waiko, a Papua New Guinean and historian, stated the wholesale desertion of the white community in many areas during the early days of the war permanently damaged white prestige and reputations among indigenous Papua New Guineans (Waiko 1991: 6). A new perspective emerged among Papua New Guineans of the Australian soldiers they encountered, a relationship that again contradicted prewar white master/black servant relationships. As Peter Ryan, an Australian intelligence officer in Papua New Guinea during the war, explained:

> a different sort of white man was seen for the first time in Australian soldiers whose humanity, informality, and willingness to labour in the sun and in the mud were in contrast to the rigid allowances of many of the pre-war residents (Ryan 1969: 534).

This new attitude towards white men that emerged under war conditions has had a lasting impact on indigenous outlooks and experiences in Papua New Guinea and Solomon Islands.

Impacts of war on village life

The Pacific War resulted in a state of confusion, dislocation of people and disruption of society throughout Solomon Islands. The arrival of the war was swift and unexpected by islanders, who lacked any knowledge of the scale of modern warfare. Many people who lived in coastal areas immediately relocated further inland when Japan invaded. Although this evacuation was ordered prior to the landing of Japanese troops on Tulagi in 1942, not all people evacuated their villages or properties and camped in the mountains. Hence, when Japanese troops advanced into Solomon Islands, panic ensued and islanders witnessed massive violence and destruction on some of their islands. Scout Abel Reka of Western Province described the impact:

> It wasn't peace. The country of Solomon Islands felt no good. It was as if we were standing in the fire. We didn't know what would happen tomorrow. We didn't know where was mother, where were the children. Running around like chickens, looking for a rock to shelter us (WPA 1988: 31).

Reka's description clearly shows the state of confusion and dislocation among indigenous people when the war reached their shores. David Gegeo of Malaita, who has done extensive research on indigenous wartime experiences, discusses the extent of social dislocation in his own Kwara'ae region of Malaita. Unlike Guadalcanal and islands of Western District, Malaita was not a centre of fighting during the campaign. A small unit of Japanese soldiers had camped at the northern end of the island but was immediately eliminated (with some taken prisoner) by the Malaitan scouts of Resident Commissioner Marchant, who had relocated the British headquarters to Auki shortly before Japanese troops invaded Tulagi. Even though Malaita did not experience a direct impact, the trauma of war still echoes among older people of Kwara'ae. Gegeo stated:

> people still talk about how women pulled their sleeping children from bed and fled into the forest with them, and how the men spent the rest of the night labouring to erect shelters in mosquito-infested swampy areas, using the dim light from burning dried bamboo and coconut leaves (Gegeo 1991: 30).

Gegeo's description of local recollections reveals how, for most islanders, the war was a challenging period. People lived in constant fear and harsh conditions. The hardship endured was physically and psychologically more far-reaching than most could ever express.

4. IMPACTS OF THE WAR

Along with dislocation, shortages of food became a struggle for local inhabitants. Food shortages were experienced mainly during Japanese invasion and occupation. Islanders were ordered beforehand by district officers to evacuate and plant new gardens further inland. Those who ignored the order were subsequently faced with food shortages. When the American troops landed on Guadalcanal, the British administration distributed rations to those villages in the greatest need as a result of the war's impact. Islanders, however, had to prove that they had planted new gardens before food could be distributed to them. This was to encourage people to remake their gardens and to ensure that military rations went only to islanders directly affected by the war as a temporary relief program.

There was also an initial loss of cash income due to the collapse of trading activity throughout the protectorate. But in contrast to these early difficulties, islanders experienced an economic rebound when the United States entered the war. This boom was due to the economic opportunities this stage of the war provided for local people and included the facilitation of small-scale economic activities such as selling of crafts, artefacts and food to the American soldiers, and a resumption (with a corresponding increase) of wages gained from labour. Although locals complained about the low wages paid to them compared to Allied troops, their monthly wages had increased at least threefold for the average labourer and over eight times for those with the rank of sergeant (Fifi'i 1991: 41). Apart from normal wages, islanders were able to sell handcrafted walking sticks, grass skirts and other crafts and food to Allied troops. Sir Frederick Osifelo, chairman of the Post-war Constitutional Committee (responsible for drafting the constitution of Solomon Islands) wrote in his autobiography of his experiences as a teenager on Malaita during the war. Osifelo recalled:

> The demand by American Marine and Army personnel for such things as sea-shell, carvings, walking-sticks, grass skirts, combs and so on, resulted in even people of my age focussing on making or finding something to sell. I was fourteen years old in 1942/1943 and actively involved in making walking-sticks, combs and grass skirts. At night we went out to the reef with torches or lit coconut leaf in search of sea-shells. Sometimes we sent our stuff to Lunga with relatives working in the Labour Corps so that they could sell them for us, at other times we sold them ourselves when the warships visited Auki (Osifelo 1985: 23).

Figure 16: Nggela people go out to trade with sailors on board the USS *Nicholas* anchored in Purvis Bay, 22 August 1943
Source: United States Navy, United States National Archives.

The war facilitated a commercial environment from which even teenagers like Osifelo benefited. Similar sentiments were expressed by Roy Kimisi, who estimated he was about 12 years old when the Americans landed on Choiseul Island. Kimisi recalled: 'I'm not sure some of those Americans cared very much about their dollars. Sometimes they'd just buy a grass skirt and throw it away' (WPA 1988: 77). Local oral recollections of the

4. IMPACTS OF THE WAR

war indicate that those who engaged in selling such things to soldiers were mostly juveniles (see Figures 16 and 17). This is perhaps because most able-bodied men were engaged in the scouting network or the labour corps. Since men were absent from their villages, women stepped up to do male chores in their families, while their children found rich rewards selling crafts to soldiers. These small-scale initiatives enhanced village-level knowledge of trade practices. They also marked the beginnings of a quest by islanders for better socioeconomic relations under the British administration. Shortly after the war ended, the Maasina Rule movement emerged with the aim of pushing for the recognition of the social welfare agenda of islanders, increased wages and the revitalisation of local cultural heritage and autonomy. Although it enjoyed limited success in achieving its objectives, it marked a significant point in the history of Solomon Islands by speeding up the decolonisation process, as discussed in the next section (Akin 2013; see also Keesing 1978).

Figure 17: Lieutenant George Rollinsk, supply officer of 193 Infantry dickers, with three natives selling canes and grass skirts, New Georgia, 2 December 1943

Source: United States Navy (photo 80-G-56673), United States National Archives.

Postwar political and economic impacts

World War II in Solomon Islands not only modified the outlooks and lifestyles of islanders, it also fuelled mounting grievances of islanders towards the colonial administration. The postwar period saw sociopolitical initiatives such as the Maasina Rule movement emerging among the local population. Maasina Rule quickly became an influential sociopolitical movement that exemplified the impact of the war on political innovation among indigenous peoples.

As discussed in the previous section, the war shone a spotlight on the racial disparities of white cultural imperialism over indigenous Solomon Islanders. Hence, shortly after hostilities subsided, the notion of Maasina Rule began to take shape. Jonathan Fifi'i, a founding member of Maasina Rule, explained in his recollection of the war that the movement developed from encounters with American troops who listened to islanders' complaints of the injustice experienced under the colonial regime, and gave advice on what indigenous people should do to express their frustrations to the British administration (Fifi'i 1988). Frederick Osifelo wrote in his biography: 'I am convinced that the war brought about the formation of Maasina Ruru [Rule]' (Osifelo 1985: 23). But Hugh Laracy argues that the roots of Maasina Rule can be dated to earlier in the history of the protectorate. The war only intensified what had been already mounting indigenous frustrations (Laracy 1983: 7). Beginning on Malaita, Maasina Rule became the first postwar sociopolitical organisation and expanded geographically to other islands. Although it was not successful in driving out the colonial regime, it made the administration painfully aware of the concerns and ambitions of its subjects, and forced these to be taken into consideration (ibid.: 6).

Maasina Rule, initially known as the 'Native Council Movement', was started in Are'are district of Malaita as early as September 1943 by the notable big man of the district, Aliki Nono'ohimae, in his village of Arairau. Nono'ohimae's vision was to set up a council to work towards the betterment of indigenous people. His early attempts had little impact due to his leaving to serve in the labour corps on Guadalcanal in 1944. Later that year, district headman Hoasihau revived the movement. Enthusiastic in his leadership, Hoasihau held meetings in Are'are with the aim of raising money to aid a chief whose responsibility would be to liaise with Europeans on matters of concern to islanders. By late 1944, Nono'ohimae returned to Malaita in time to team up with Hoasihau to promote the Native Council Movement. His encounter with American troops during his time at the labour corps camp on Guadalcanal bolstered his belief in local governance by islanders.

By mid-1945, the Native Council Movement, which now bore the name 'Maasina Rule' or 'the rule of brotherhood', gained momentum throughout Malaita, following a 'patrol' led by Nori, another Are'are man and returned member of the labour corps who shared the movement's leadership. The movement continued to gain popularity and, by December 1945, the first order was issued on Malaita forbidding Malaitans to accept labour recruitment for Europeans. Early the following year, the making of communal farms and construction of new coastal villages began. On 26 December 1945, Maasina Rule was formally established with 5,000 members and nine council members. In 1947, a large number of people were relocated to the newly built communally owned coastal villages. By then, the movement had spread to the islands of Ulawa, San Cristobal (Makira) and Guadalcanal. In late June 1947, Maasina Rule leaders and 7,000 supporters met at Auki on Malaita with the district commissioner. One of the explicit demands expressed during the meeting was for an increase in islanders' wages to 12 pounds per annum: a demand originally made in the prewar period and that lingered during the war. On 31 August 1947, threatened by its popularity among islanders, the British regime executed 'Operation De-Louse' in an effort to put a stop to the movement. By early 1948, all accused members of Maasina Rule were tried and imprisoned (Laracy 1983: 17–20). The designated name for the operation is itself an indication of the colonial mentality and the administration's contempt for islanders who had contributed so much to the Allied victory, and their efforts to voice their concerns and grievances.

The origins of Maasina Rule on Malaita are significant for understanding the geographical area it covered and its legitimacy among its followers. Both founders of the movement, Nono'ohimae and Hoasihau, were from the Are'are district of Malaita and had been members of the Fallowes movement. This movement was one of a series of attempts to call upon the British administration to address, or at least listen to, the grievances of islanders in the 1930s. The Fallowes movement was organised by an Anglican missionary, Richard Fallowes, from the mid to late 1930s, and gained momentum particularly on the islands of Isabel and Nggela. Fallowes observed that the government failed to take heed of the interests of those it governed, concerning itself only with the interests of the few

European settlers in the protectorate. His aim was to form a parliament that would represent islanders in discussing matters of interest to the government — a concept resembling the Native Council Movement initiated by Nono'ohimae and Hoasihau (Laracy 1983: 13–14). Fallowes was later deported, but his legacy left an imprint among many islanders.

Although Nono'ohimae was pagan, five of the nine council members were teachers of the South Seas Evangelical Mission (now known as the South Seas Evangelical Church, or SSEC). The SSEC had its first contact with indigenous labourers in Queensland in 1886 (it was then known as the Queensland Kanaka Mission). In 1904, the SSEC established its mission headquarters on Malaita, spreading throughout Malaita and Makira where Maasina Rule was also widely accepted. The remaining four members of the council were either pagan or from other Christian denominations (Laracy 1983: 20). In the western Solomons, where the people were evangelised by the Methodist Mission Society, Maasina Rule was only a distant echo and had no influence. On Guadalcanal, the ideology of Maasina Rule was introduced by the local war hero Sergeant Major Jacob Vouza, but was short-lived after he was arrested in 1947 alongside other members of the movement (ibid.: 23). Yet again, the scale of the Maasina Rule movement indicated the widespread demand by islanders for representation and improvement in their welfare under the British administration, which might not have been felt, or at least not have been felt so strongly, without encountering and being encouraged by Allied troops during the war.

Commercial centralisation

The war also opened new avenues for economic development. The protectorate benefited immensely from the relocation of its administrative headquarters from Tulagi to Honiara after 1953. Infrastructure such as roads, bridges, Quonset huts, the military hospital and airfields became the foundation for postwar economic reconstruction in the protectorate.

One major infrastructural product of the war was the Solomon Islands international airport. Henderson Field, as it was originally called, was initially built by Japanese troops on Guadalcanal shortly after their invasion of Tulagi (the British protectorate headquarters until February 1942). On 7 August 1942, threatened by the construction of the airfield, the United States First Marine Division made its historic landing on Guadalcanal. The airfield was captured on 8 August and was named

Henderson Field after Major Crofton Henderson, a marine aviator who was killed at the Battle of Midway (Jersey 2008: xiv). The airfield was reopened in 1969 as the Solomon Islands international airport, retaining the name Henderson Airport.[1]

Besides the historic Henderson Field, roads built by the Allied forces are still used today, and Quonset huts built for military purposes have long been used by various government authorities who now own the properties on which the huts are located. The Public Works Department used to house a few offices in these historic huts, but in 2014 all the huts were demolished to make way for new developments. This military infrastructure, now decaying, formed the basis for economic development and reconstruction of economic activities in the former protectorate.

Honiara became the centre of all major economic activities in the postwar period. The British administration did not anticipate the long-term consequences of centralising development on Guadalcanal. Since the war had already laid an infrastructural foundation to rebuild the protectorate, it was considered logical to use what was already in place. However, the centralisation of economic activities on Guadalcanal began to pose another difficulty: a surge of rural–urban migration and the appearance of related social problems. The British administration at the time could not foresee the impact these would have on islanders over 50 years, blinkered perhaps by the convenience of infrastructure established during the war. Consequently, in 1998, 20 years after Solomon Islands gained independence from Britain, the country experienced an ethnic confrontation between people of Malaita and Guadalcanal. Among other causes of the conflict was the frustration of Guadalcanal people over the growing numbers of Malaitans migrating to their island as

---

1   In 2000, the Japanese Government funded the renovation of Henderson Airport, and Japanese consultants suggested a change to the historic Allied name of the airport. Perhaps in an attempt to show appreciation for the continual support of the Japanese Government in maintaining the airport, the Solomon Islands Government made a public announcement that it would rename Henderson Airport to 'Honiara International Airport'. The announcement resulted in an online petition opposing the change with over 8,000 signatures, as well as official exchanges between the Solomon Islands Government and United States diplomats. In 2003, when the terminal renovations were completed, Prime Minister Allan Kemakeza announced that the airport will be officially known as 'Honiara International Airport — Henderson Field' (ABC Radio Australia 2012; see also usmarineraiders.org/about-the-raiders/history/combat-operations/guadalcanal/thank-you-note-from-solomon-island-prime-minister/).

a result of the 'pull' factors of economic development and urbanisation. John Naitoro (2000: 7) argued that the historical cause of the unrest is rooted in development centralisation on Guadalcanal.

The legacy of the war not only posed long-term hurdles to the political and economic development of Solomon Islands, it also provided an avenue for long-term economic benefits from remnants of military artillery and other wreckage, at both the national and local levels. The islands of Guadalcanal, Nggela and Western Province, where large-scale military confrontations took place, have become giant museums for international visitors. Left in situ in the landscape rather than gathered into a modern museum collection, the physical fragments of war have become a source of income to customary landowners, who charge small fees to visitors of battle sites within their jurisdiction. Battlefield tours to historical sites such as Bloody Ridge, Henderson Field and Beach Red are conducted for international visitors and descendants of Allied soldiers who participated in the war.[2] On 7 August of each year, United States Marines and other veterans of the war and their descendants return to Solomon Islands to celebrate the initial landing of the First Marine Division on Guadalcanal and conduct commemoration ceremonies for fallen comrades. Although international visitors to Solomon Islands are few compared to sites such as the Kokoda Trail in Papua New Guinea, the economic platform the war has established is still considerable.

Conclusion

The war had immediate and long-lasting influences on indigenous islanders' social world views and on economic and political events at both local and national levels. Islanders began to perceive their social environment differently and glimpsed the world beyond their borders. As Allied troops entered the war, the 'master–boy' relationship was shaken and the opportunity to interact with white men (American GIs) emerged. This provided a lesson enabling islanders to become more critically aware of and contest their supposed racial inferiority so entrenched

---

2 John Innes, a historian of the Guadalcanal Battlefield, conducts battlefield tours annually on Guadalcanal and Tulagi. In 2011, in collaboration with the Solomon Scouts and Coastwatchers Trust, his field tour on Guadalcanal was documented by the Solomon Islands Broadcasting Corporation (Audio) and Trad Records (a local company in Honiara), who produced a DVD of the tour (Innes 2013). All the recordings are in the author's possession but can also be purchased from the Solomon Scouts and Coastwatchers Trust.

by white 'masters' in the prewar protectorate. Although islanders had expressed their grievances prior to the war, their consciousness of the injustice of subjection to authority was heightened when a sudden shift of interracial interaction occurred. Having become convinced and more confident of their rights to better conditions, islanders openly criticised the British regime in the postwar period. One method of protesting their dissatisfaction with the colonial administration was through the formation of the Maasina Rule movement, which was eventually broken up by the British colonial authorities in 1947. However, its formation ensured that islanders' grievances were outlined and their voices heard. Beyond these social and political impacts, the war also provided economic opportunities from which Solomon Islands still benefits. Despite creating unforeseen social tension from rural–urban migration, the country benefited from wartime military infrastructure, and the physical remnants of the war have provided long-term economic gains to local peoples as well as contributing to the national economy of the country. They have also contributed costs, and it is to these I turn in the chapter that follows.

5
Monument-building and Nation-building

Beyond the dedication of the statue of Sir Jacob Vouza in 1992, it has taken almost 70 years for the efforts of Solomon Islanders who participated in the Pacific Campaign of World War II to be recognised and celebrated. On 7 August 2011, the anniversary of the United States Marine Corps' landing on Guadalcanal, a monument was unveiled and handed over to the people of Solomon Islands by the governor general, Sir Frank Kabui.

At the entrance to Honiara's central jetty at the seaward end of Commonwealth Street stands this long-overdue monument honouring the legacy of Solomon Islanders and Allied coastwatchers who participated in the war effort on Guadalcanal and elsewhere. Designed and sculpted by the celebrated local artist Frank Haikiu, the monument features four life-sized figures on a 2-metre-high plinth, representing three islanders and a European (Figure 18). The two scouts are shirtless and dressed only in khaki shorts while holding bush knives and .303 rifles. This is an accurate representation of the dress code of their time. Radio operators, on the other hand, were trained personnel and were slightly higher in rank than the scouts. Hence, the artist impression of the radio operator having a shirt on is an accurate depiction of their status in the scouting network's hierarchy. Amid the three islanders is a well-dressed European-looking male, with a hat and binoculars, looking out to sea. This figure represents a coastwatcher, symbolically scanning the horizon with his binoculars for any suspicious or subversive developments throughout the islands. This monument, now known as the Pride of Our Nation, was the first major phase of the Solomon Scouts and Coastwatchers Trust's monument-building initiative.

Figure 18: Artist Frank Haikiu's design of the Pride of Our Nation sculpture, 2009
Source: Solomon Scouts and Coastwatchers Trust.

A year later, on the 70th anniversary of the United States Marines' landing, the second phase of the project was completed. An honour roll was unveiled, listing on two plinths at the back of the monument the names of those who served in the British Solomon Islands Defence Force, including local scouts and coastwatchers. The final phase of the monument project was completed in early August 2013, with the dedication of a memorial anchor in honour of the Royal Australian Navy (Figure 19). In front of the anchor is a plaque that bears a brief historical description of the coastwatching network and its relationship to islanders who served as scouts during the Allied–Japanese confrontation in Solomon Islands. At the final monument dedication, the project coordinator, Bruce Saunders, announced in his speech that 'the story is complete; the Pride of Our Nation is complete' (Saunders 2013).

5. MONUMENT-BUILDING AND NATION-BUILDING

Together, the Solomon scouts and coastwatchers memorial, the honour roll and the Royal Australian Navy monument were given the official title the 'Pride of Our Nation' monument.

Eric Feldt, commander of the coastwatchers throughout the Pacific War began his book *The Coastwatchers* by stating that the coastwatchers 'played a vital part in these operations, a part so important that without them the whole course of the war in the Pacific would have been drastically changed' (Feldt 1991: 1). Feldt's statement is similar in sentiment to Halsey's quotation on the plinth of the Honiara monument (see Chapter 1). Evident in these sorts of statements is that the coastwatchers became a focus of early celebration and remembrance of the Allied victory in Solomon Islands. But the tales of the scouts, who formed the backbone of the coastwatchers, have not been consistently passed on in the islands over the ensuing decades, gradually becoming part of a forgotten national past. It is this forgotten past that the Pride of Our Nation monument attempts to revive. This chapter discusses the planning and building of the monument, why it is important and relevant to the contemporary Solomon Islands and what it has achieved to date. As Susanne Küchler (1999: 53) has shown, 'a culture without monuments appears to us like a ship lost to the sea — unable to navigate and correct mistaken judgement'.

Figure 19: The Pride of Our Nation monument

This image shows the three elements that make up the completed monument. The two white plinths behind the coastwatchers' statue are the honour rolls, while the black anchor at the right is the Royal Australian Navy monument.

Source: Photo by Anna Kwai.

Monuments and commemoration in Solomon Islands

Monuments and commemorations are not foreign concepts in the traditional societies of Solomon Islands, but the modern practice of constructing monuments or sculptures in public spaces with the sociopolitical intention of nation-building and of strengthening collective interests has made these aspects of the culture seem new. As a child, I grew up in a traditional village setting where the oldest generation of the village were grandchildren of a pagan *fata'abu* or priest, who decided to abandon his pagan god for the new Christian god, introduced to him by his coastal relatives. But even after generations of Christianity, when passing certain places in the bush, people today still fall silent because of the heaviness of the past that dwells around them. These sites each have a tale, perhaps marking the spot where a leader died during a tribal skirmish, or the corpse of a priest was left to decay before his bones were moved to his final resting place. Women and girls are not allowed to pass through some sites. Although as a child I did not understand the stories behind the sacredness of these objects or sites, I knew that they were revered. These are monuments that each tribal group associates with an event or a traditional political figure. In her study of the practice of *malanggan*, a ceremony marking the finishing of the work of the dead in the Bismarck Archipelago, Papua New Guinea, Küchler noted:

> We may fail to recognise such objects [artworks embedded in the culture] as monuments as their perishability and fleeting presence in culture conflict with our [Western] assumption that commemorative work should provide a lasting visual referent for acts of remembrance, yet it is their ephemerality that allows us to understand the place of memory in modern culture, best exemplified by the war memorial (Küchler 1999: 55).

The Japanese Memorial and the Guadalcanal American Memorial

The twentieth-century phenomenon of war monument–building began in Solomon Islands only in the early 1980s. The Japanese returned, but this time to unveil a monument commemorating their comrades who fell during the battles of Guadalcanal. On Mount Austen east of Honiara (known to the Allies as Hill 35), stands this Japanese memorial (Figure 20). The monument consists of two white plinths facing seaward, looking down on significant battle sites such as Henderson Field, the Galloping Horse and the Seahorse. The monument itself was built on the north-west end of the ridge where the Battle of the Gifu was fought.[1] Near the entrance of the monument is a sculpture of the Japanese artist Seiichi Takahashi, who was killed in combat on Guadalcanal, and over his shoulder is a fishing net. The Takahashi sculpture was donated by the city of Ishinomaki where he was born.

Figure 20: Japanese War Memorial
Source: Solomon Scouts and Coastwatchers Trust.

Eight years after the dedication of the Japanese memorial, the Guadalcanal American Memorial was unveiled on Skyline Ridge (or Hill 73) (Figure 21). In what seemed a war of monument-building, the American memorial was built almost parallel to the Japanese memorial at Mount Austen. The Guadalcanal American Memorial was initiated in the early 1990s through the cooperative effort of the Guadalcanal Solomon Islands War Memorial Foundation and the American Battle Monument Commission. The site was chosen primarily for its spectacular views, again overlooking some of the significant battlegrounds on Guadalcanal. Engraved on marble plinths are detailed accounts of the phases of the battle of Guadalcanal. Adding to the historical significance of the site, during its excavation in early 1992

---

1 The battle was named Gifu by the Japanese defenders involved since most of these soldiers were from the town of Gifu Prefecture in the Chubu region of central Japan.

the remains of an unknown Allied soldier were discovered in a shallow grave on the hill. When the monument was constructed, a star-shaped plaque was placed within the compound in honour of this 'unknown warrior'. The remains were later identified as belonging to Sergeant John Branic of the United States Marine Corps. The Guadalcanal American Memorial was unveiled on 7 August 1992, to mark the 50th anniversary of the United States Marines' landing on Guadalcanal, and a ceremony continues to be held at the monument on the same day every year. Beyond mourning the dead and celebrating victory in the Solomons Campaign, the United States monument is historically significant since it also marks the first American offensive in World War II.

Figure 21: Guadalcanal American Memorial, 2017
Source: Solomon Scouts and Coastwatchers Trust.

Since its dedication in 1984, the Japanese memorial has only occasionally been the site of Japanese commemorative ceremonies. In 2008, a Japanese bone recovery mission was conducted and this led to ceremonies being held at the monument, including Shinto rituals, wreath laying and a flag-raising ceremony (*Solomon Times Online* 2008). Recovered bones of Japanese soldiers were burnt in front of the monument and the ashes returned to Japan.

In contrast, the American monument has been a site of regular commemoration. Since its unveiling in 1992, the monument has annually hosted veterans, international dignitaries, officials and representatives of the United States Marines. The annual 7 August program begins at

6:55 am with the arrival of the Solomon Islands prime minister and governor general, followed by a flag-raising ceremony, speeches and laying of wreaths. The day's program concludes at the Honiara Yacht Club, where a memorial plaque lies in honour of Douglas Munro, a member of the United States Coast Guard, mortally wounded on Guadalcanal in September 1942. While the 7 August ceremony at the Skyline Ridge memorial is a private commemoration organised for American veterans, over the years it has been attended by officials of the Solomon Islands Government as well as local residents.

Sir Jacob Vouza statue

Neither the Japanese nor American memorials on Guadalcanal seem to have any connection to a past — whether horrific or victorious — that is shared with the indigenous inhabitants of the land on which they stand. The Japanese memorial serves the purpose of mourning loss rather than celebrating victory, so perhaps some form of acknowledgement of islanders' contributions would have been more appropriate for the American memorial, in light of the local contribution to the Allied victory. Michael Rowland argues that in order for a 'monument' to become a 'memorial', it must fulfil three functions: (1) acknowledge the importance of the dead and their sacrificial deeds, (2) accept the loss in a collective manner and substitute a gain for it through symbolic objects and (3) identify the dead through remembering names in rolls of honour and commemorative events (Rowland 1999: 144). But these functions at the American memorial do not seem to encompass islanders' efforts. In an effort to fill the gap of recognising islanders' contributions, a bronze sculpture of local war hero Sir Jacob Vouza was built at the same time as the American monument. A major portion of the funds for the construction of the monuments were donated in 1989 by a United States congressional appropriation, and the American Battle Monuments Commission to the Solomon Islands Memorial Foundation (White 1995: 539).

The bronze statue was made in Australia and shipped to Honiara in July 1990. It was initially planned to be part of the American Guadalcanal Memorial at Skyline ridge. However, since funding for the American memorial came directly from the United States, the appropriateness of Vouza's statue to be placed within its physical confines was reconsidered. This led to the location of Vouza's statue to the Rove police headquarters.

The individualisation of the Vouza sculpture does not go unnoticed by Solomon Islanders. The former prime minister, the late Sir Peter Kenilorea, wrote to the *Solomon Star* criticising the development:

> The Second World War was not our war and Sir Jacob Vouza's proposed statue is a form of 'grease' by Americans to allow the Solomon Islands Government to accommodate the memorial ... What possible benefits do we, as a country get out of the War Memorial? This simply reinforces local peoples' sense of inferiority. The idea to build the monument, its design, the money and the technology all belong to foreigners ... And yet again, at the height of Skyline Ridge we have yet to witness another battle between USA and Japan. Do we need them to do that yet again in our own soils? ... I think that apart from the praise given to our people for their services during the war years, the Americans and British need to consider some form of compensations to our local people ... I think we have already had enough of USA vs Japan during the last war (*Solomon Star* 28 April 1989: 7, cited in White 1995: 538).[2]

The Vouza sculpture is a life-size figure of the hero, standing on a marble plinth with a bush knife in his right hand, looking out to the coast (Figure 22). At the rear of the statue are two white pillars with details of all Allied military units that took part in the battle for Solomon Islands. On the front of the plinth are the words 'America, Australia, New Zealand and their Allies thank the Solomon Islanders for their tremendous World War II effort. This statue honours all Solomon Islanders who fought alongside us during the Solomon Island battles from Guadalcanal to Bougainville'.

Despite this, the individualised nature of the Vouza sculpture means it fails to collectively remember or represent all local veterans. As Rowland (1999: 130) discusses, certain memorials are 'successful by the demands they make for recognition of what was done, to whom and by whom'. The Vouza memorial is successful in promoting an individual tale of heroism but suppresses the recognition of other islanders who were equally heroic in the war. When studying British memorials to World War I, Alex King (1999) also revealed that the choices made in designing a memorial involve the erasure of certain memories. Despite the general inscription on the Vouza monument acknowledging all Solomon Islanders, the use of a single iconic individual does not offer any connection to other local veterans or

---

2 Note that Sir Peter Kenilorea was chairman of the Solomon Scouts and Coastwatchers Trust when it was founded in 2009.

their families, and the statue stands idle as if without purpose and notice in central Honiara. Hence, the recognition owed to the islander war effort has remained obscure. In order to address this shortfall in memory, the idea of the Pride of Our Nation monument was conceived.

Figure 22: Sir Jacob Vouza monument, 2013
Source: Photo by Anna Kwai.

The Solomon Scouts and Coastwatchers Trust

The initial idea for a monument in honour of Solomon Islanders came from Australian expatriate and businessman Sir Bruce Saunders KBE OBE, who has lived in Solomon Islands for over 40 years. Saunders first arrived in Solomon Islands in 1968 after marrying his wife Keithie, a daughter of Alvin Blum, a United States serviceman in the Solomons Campaign who returned to Guadalcanal after the war as a missionary for the Baha'i faith (Saunders 2013). The close family connection to and identification with Solomon Islands, and a strong interest in war histories, has seen Saunders regularly visiting battle sites on Guadalcanal and elsewhere in the islands since his arrival in the country. In 1972, Saunders and his family established a tour business to administer to wartime veterans of both American and Japanese soldiers who return to visit Solomon Islands.

This exposure to the history of the Solomons Campaign and visiting veterans has increased Saunders' knowledge of the significance of local contributions to the war effort in the Solomons Campaign. He stated:

> I was always impressed by the fact that when people spoke about the war they always talked about what a Solomon Scout did — a Scout was always referred to as a 'Solomon Scout', not a scout from Guadalcanal, from Vela la Vela etc. I was also aware that the victory of the Guadalcanal Campaign for the Allies was due to a great extent on the work of the Coastwatchers and the Solomon Scouts (Solomon Scouts and Coastwatchers Memorial Trust 2010).

With this in mind, and having remained in the country to endure the 1998–2002 ethnic unrest and witness a young nation struggling to recover from major sociopolitical upheaval, Saunders conceived of building a monument to herald local wartime contributions and also to serve as a bridge to promote national unity and identity for a nation struggling to recover from turmoil. Saunders brought his idea to the attention of Prime Minister Derek Silkua, and on 7 August 2009 the Guadalcanal War Memorial Trust was founded and formally endorsed by the Solomon Islands Government.[3] The trust board originally comprised seven members: Sir Bruce Saunders, founder of the trust; Sir Peter Kenilorea, the first prime minister;[4] John Innes, a historian of the Guadalcanal campaign; Keithie Saunders, the United States consular agent to Solomon Islands; Anna Kwai; Michael Ben, secretary of the Solomon Islands Veterans Association; and Michael Liliau, a member of parliament for Guadalcanal Province and the son of local scout Bruno Nana (Aruhuri 2003).[5] The incorporation of such a variety of members into the trust board is significant for understanding the momentum gained by the project across different groups of people in the broader society of Solomon Islands, and its success in raising public awareness of the national pride and unification agenda of the Pride of Our Nation monument. In a press conference organised by the trust in early 2010, Saunders explained that with the country struggling to create a national identity, there was no specific recognition of the service rendered by the Solomon scouts

---

3 See Appendix 1: Prime Minister Derek Sikua's letter of endorsement of the Solomon Scouts and Coastwatchers Trust.
4 Sir Peter Kenilorea died in February 2016.
5 Bruno Nana died in late 2011. His daughter has transcribed his wartime stories into a booklet.

and coastwatchers in the Pacific War. The building of a monument to recognise the services of the Solomon scouts and coastwatchers could help to restore a sense of pride and national identity.

By early 2011, a site was chosen and approved by the Honiara City Council and local artist Frank Haikiu was given the task of designing and building the monument. At the entrance to the Solomon Islands Ports Authority, at the end of Commonwealth Street in the heart of Honiara, a groundbreaking ceremony took place on 26 May 2011. The site was chosen not for any particular historical purpose, but for a sociopolitical need. Commonwealth Street is one of the busiest streets in Honiara and is used by heavy vehicles heading to and from the national port compound. It is also a major public thoroughfare leading to the national jetty, the access point for inter-island travel to and from Honiara.

The placement of the monument on such a busy street will hopefully minimise any acts of vandalism and make maintenance more convenient. As Alex King argues, a physical memorial requires regular care to ensure its durability: 'no monument can resist the effect of time and nature, and the effectiveness of a memorial demands not only investment in its structure, but also a commitment to its upkeep' (King 1999: 151). This was of course a factor the trust board discussed when choosing the site. For the designer, Frank Haikiu, the site would also convey the purpose of the monument to all Solomon Islanders: 'I want all Solomon Islanders coming in and going out of Honiara to look at this monument and think, "that could be my grandfather, father or relative" and feel a sense of pride for what Solomon Islanders did during the war' (Figure 23).[6]

In his speech at the dedication ceremony, Sir Peter Kenilorea, the nation's first prime minister and a member of the trust board, said that the site was chosen carefully, remarking 'the figures look northwards to the sea, and they will welcome Solomon Islanders travelling to the capital from their homes in the islands. For those travelling home, the figures will wish them a safe journey after their time in Honiara' (Kenilorea 2011).

---

6 Frank Haikiu's message was delivered by Bruce Saunders during the unveiling of the monument in 2011. Although Frank attended the ceremony, he did not speak. A recording of his message as spoken by Sir Bruce is in the author's possession and can also be obtained from the Solomon Islands Broadcasting Corporation library in Honiara. On 7 August 2015, during a commemoration ceremony at Commonwealth Street, a plaque was unveiled in honour of artist Frank Haikiu. The plaque was placed on the forefront plinth of the monument.

Figure 23: Frank Haikiu (second from left) with Solomon Scouts and Coastwatchers Trust Medal recipient Sebastian Ilala and members of the Australian military during the 2015 ceremony at Commonwealth Street, Honiara
Source: Courtesy of Greg Terrill.

But the trust not only invests in building monuments. As mentioned, the role of Solomon Islanders in the coastwatching network, while instrumental to the Allied victory, had faded in island memories of the war. This was due in part to the submission of local memories to dominant forms of histories. Geoffrey White (1995: 533) argued that 'when local stories do emerge in the public spaces of national memory, they risk being so disfigured by dominant narratives and commodifying practices that they become unrecognizable'. This is true of Solomon Islanders' participation in the war. In the period after the war, local memories became less significant among dominant narratives of Allied exploits in the Pacific theatre so that even a general knowledge of local experiences and exploits was dying as each older generation passed away. And because the local culture is vested in oral recollections, as the decades passed, those memories gradually faded. Written narratives were not available until the 1980s, when researchers and educated Solomon Islanders started to record and translate the wartime recollections of surviving veterans (see Aruhuri 2003; Bennett 1988; Gegeo 1988; WPA 1988).

The iconography of the sculpture itself is reflective of the submission of local knowledge to popular narratives. Influenced by these dominant narratives, the sculptor crafted the European figure to be taller than the local figures: a depiction that unintentionally downplays the efforts of islanders during the war. Furthermore, this depiction reflects the racial hierarchy that existed among 'white' colonial officers and 'black natives' during the war, sentiments that still exist in the country.

To ensure that younger generations are aware of the wartime contributions of their ancestors, the memorial project, through its educational objective, pushed for inclusion of local war histories into the secondary school curriculum, and drew high school students into the project through a poster competition and school awareness programs. In early 2013, a brief story of the roles of islanders in the Solomons Campaign finally found a place in the revised Year 8 history textbook (Daudau et al. 2013: 27–50). Working in partnership with the curriculum department through the Ministry of Education and Human Resources Development, the project has partially achieved its vision of pushing the story of Solomon scouts and coastwatchers to the fore, in the realisation that in order for national pride and unity to be fostered by the monument, the story needs to be told. One way to ensure this is to place it into the school curriculum. In the following years, the textbook was made available to schools across Solomon Islands. Although the scouts and coastwatchers story is summarised in a mere quarter page among numerous history topics, it is still significant in retelling forgotten stories of local war experiences to the younger generations.

The Pride of Our Nation and contemporary Solomon Islands

As argued by T.G. Ashplant, Graham Dawson and Michael Roper in *The Politics of War Memory and Commemoration* (2000: 3–85), there are two principal approaches in the literature on war memory and commemorations, entailing either a psychological or political emphasis. In the psychological view, monuments are where surviving veterans and relatives gather to remember the dead, and their wartime memories are reconciled. From a political standpoint, monuments recognised national pasts in the light of modern socio-political and economic developments. The Pride of Our Nation monument has become the site of a collective memory of a triumphant but difficult past, one that was shared with the

Allied nations. Susanne Küchler (1999: 55) shows that war memorials enable different memories to come together despite their conflicting natures. For the few local surviving veterans of the war, the monument is a place to remember both the good and bad experiences the war brought to their shores and their lives. But the monument is also a place where islanders' participation is acknowledged by the international community. For people like Baroness Ann Taylor, head of delegation of the Commonwealth Parliamentary Association of the United Kingdom, a gesture of respect for the commitment of islanders to the British Solomon Islands administration during the dark days of the war is the appropriate message to relay when laying a wreath at the new monument. During the ceremony in 2013, her wreath bore the message: 'In grateful memory, rest in peace. All members and staff, Houses of Parliament, United Kingdom' (NPSI 2013) (Figure 24).

Figure 24: Rt Hon. Baroness Ann Taylor lays a wreath at the Pride of Our Nation monument

Source: Solomon Islands National Parliament Media Department.

In 1998, 20 years after obtaining political autonomy from Great Britain, the young nation of Solomon Islands faced a sociopolitical clash between the people of the provinces of Guadalcanal and Malaita. Among the causes of the tension were the grievances by Malaitans of commercial centralisation on Guadalcanal, which had its roots in the postwar exploitation of Allied infrastructure by the British administration, and the demand by the people of Guadalcanal that all Malaitans on Guadalcanal leave their island and return lands, whether purchased legally or not. The situation escalated as paramilitary groups were organised by both sides. For four years (1998–2002) the country was in turmoil, with over 22,000 Malaitans and people from other provinces fleeing the capital for their home islands (Bennett 2002). Although peace was restored in 2003 through an Australian-led joint effort by Pacific nations, the Regional Assistance Mission to Solomon Islands (RAMSI), the country still struggles to recover politically, economically and socially. Recognising the wartime contributions of islanders by constructing the monument is an invaluable step, symbolically depicting a nationally unifying image of islanders working together during the war.

The Pride of Our Nation monument is the first of its kind in the country. Sculpted by a local artist, built locally and dedicated to the people of Solomon Islands, there is a more immediate sense of public connection to it than to other existing monuments. After the 2011 commemoration ceremony in Honiara, I walked among the crowd on Commonwealth Street asking individuals of their impressions of the newly erected monument. All the people I spoke to expressed their appreciation for recognising the effort of islanders in the war. Other positive sentiments included that the monument beautifies the capital and provides a site for tourists to visit. But these acknowledgements of the monument's value do not prevent different interpretations of the physical monument itself. Drawing upon the country's relationship with RAMSI, trust board member Sir Peter Kenilorea stated in his 2011 speech that the monument 'is also a reminder that the united purpose and spirit of cooperation among the Coastwatchers from Australia, Great Britain and New Zealand — alongside the Solomon Scouts of the time — laid the foundations on which the spirit of RAMSI has become evident in the past several years. Everyone working together for the benefit of all' (Kenilorea 2011). In the editorial section of the *Solomon Star*, one Honiara resident thanked those who conceived the idea of building the monument, concluding 'this is our pride and may the story of these men live through the ages in this monument' (Aquilani 2011).

The Pride of Our Nation monument: A national success

The Solomon Scouts and Coastwatchers Trust has been successful in gaining recognition on national and international fronts. In 2010, the Royal Solomon Islands Police Force announced that the year's recruits (the '2010 recruit wing') would be named 'Solomon Scouts and Coastwatchers', a significant gesture towards ensuring the legacy of the local wartime effort prevails. The recruit wing continues to provide a guard of honour alongside members of the United States Marine Corps at the yearly commemoration ceremonies.

The erection of the Pride of Our Nation monument has seen the 7 August commemoration at the American monument shift from a private ceremony to a national celebration. In 2011, for the first time, a series of ceremonies was held, organised to include the local Solomon Islands public and coinciding with the American memorial program. The 2011 program began at the American memorial, moved to Commonwealth Street for the unveiling of the Pride of Our Nation monument and finished at the Munro plaque at the Yacht Club.

The official dedication ceremony began with the arrival of the Solomon Islands governor general, followed by words of welcome from the organisers. An opening prayer was said by Bishop David Vunagi of the Anglican Church. Peter Kenilorea, the chairman of the monument trust board, then gave a speech on behalf of the trust, followed by speeches from the Royal Australian Navy adviser, Commander Geoff Turner, and Colonel Robert Loyne of the United States Marine Corps. The monument was then unveiled by the governor general and wreaths were laid by various dignitaries. A Christian dedication ritual was performed around the monument by the bishop, and the ceremony was concluded with a closing prayer by Timothy Lufuia of the Baha'i faith. During the public street celebration that followed, various groups performed, including the United States Marine Corps Band, church groups and local artists. A public exhibit was also hosted by the Solomon Islands National Museum and later relocated to the museum.[7] The ceremony was coordinated by the Reverend Mareta Tahu of the Methodist Church.

---

7   The events on 7 August 2011 were documented live by the Solomon Islands Broadcasting Corporation and a DVD was produced and made available for purchase by the trust board.

The incorporation of different Christian denominations and other groups in the street celebration was a significant achievement for the monument's aim of promoting a sense of national unity and identity.

The event on 7 August 2011 was indeed a day of national celebration. Around the new monument were crowds of people trying to get a glimpse of the figures on the monument, or read the inscriptions on the plinth. In my quest for public feedback on the monument, I stood among the crowd listening to the comments of ordinary people on what they saw and thought of the sculptures. There was a sense of admiration, but also curious questions such as whether the life-sized figures were depictions of individual islanders — an impression that perhaps stemmed from the understanding of the Vouza statue. As a member of the project's organising committee, it was a relief to see from a distance the designer, Frank Haikiu, explaining his vision for the monument and stating that the figures did not represent any particular individuals.

International recognition

Since the dedication in 2011, the annual Pride of Our Nation commemoration ceremony has attracted the local public, international dignitaries, veterans and families of veterans of Guadalcanal, as well the international media. In 2010, a team from Maori Television in New Zealand filmed a documentary featuring Aaron Kumana, one of the surviving veterans who rescued the future United States president John F. Kennedy and his crew when PT-109 sank after a collision with a Japanese destroyer off Naru Island. The documentary was aired in New Zealand during Anzac Week in 2011.

In 2012, to mark the 70th anniversary of the United States Marine Corps' landing on Guadalcanal, President Barack Obama sent a letter of recognition for the roles played by Solomon Islanders in the Pacific Campaign, writing 'their efforts helped save the Pacific, and they are worthy of the highest praise and recognition' (see Appendix 2). Such recognition reflects the significance of islander contributions to the war effort throughout Solomon Islands and aids in spreading the message of national pride and unity that the monuments portrays. A few weeks after the 70th anniversary celebrations, William and Catherine, the Duke and Duchess of Cambridge, reopened the newly upgraded Commonwealth Street and inspected the Pride of Our Nation monument in a gesture of recognition from Buckingham Palace (Figure 25).

Figure 25: The Duke and Duchess of Cambridge at the reopening of Commonwealth Street, 2012
Source: Solomon Scouts and Coastwatchers Trust.

In 2013, the Australian Government formally paid tribute to the Solomon scouts and coastwatchers' efforts in the war. This recognition included the provision of 500 commemorative medallions, officially handed over by the Australian Parliamentary Secretary for Defence, David Feeney. During a small gathering in Honiara, Feeney acknowledged Solomon Islanders' contributions to the Royal Australian Navy's coastwatching network and admitted that it was an overdue gesture by the Australian Government and 'the first ever award of the Solomon Islands Coastwatcher and Scouts medallion' (Armbruster 2013). Sadly, the *Solomon Star* (2013: 3) reported 'the commemorative medallions are too late for most old soldiers. Only three remain and none could attend. Edward Lulumani, one of the surviving veterans, died only a week before the medallions were awarded'.

A year later, the United States Secretary of State John Kerry laid a wreath at the monument as a political gesture of appreciation of the service of Solomon Islanders to the Allied war efforts. In 2015, four-star General Vincent K. Brooks, commanding general of the United States Army Pacific, also paid tribute at the monument during a diplomatic visit to Honiara, laying a wreath in honour of those who served. The monument has become a de rigueur stop for political dignitaries visiting the country to pay tribute to the lives that were lost and the hardships faced by those affected in World War II.

Conclusion

The Solomon Scouts and Coastwatchers Trust has filled a gap in the history of the Solomons Campaign of World War II, and also a gap in memory-making and monument-building in the country. The project ensured that a fading piece of the nation's history was revived for the benefit of the present and future generations. Through its educational component, knowledge of a heroic tale will prevail among the younger population of the country and national pride and identity will be found in the collective efforts of Solomon Islanders who served with the Allies during the war. Through and beyond this, the Pride of Our Nation monument is becoming an agent for national unity, and serves as a reminder of the long-term impacts the war had on a developing nation. The war helped bring about the centralisation of development through the immediate availability of infrastructure in the postwar period. This, in part, contributed to the upheavals that began in 1998. Yet while the monument recognises a heroic legacy and promotes national identity, it does not capture the complexities of war as endured by islanders during the campaign, nor does it acknowledge the widows and children of those who served.

6

Conclusion

The arrival of World War II in the British Solomon Islands Protectorate in early 1942 was neither sought nor anticipated by the indigenous population. Local understandings of the outside world were limited. The war had nothing to do with the local inhabitants of the protectorate but was fought between Japan and the Allied nations on indigenous land. The forms of military conduct practised by Western countries were alien to local understanding of warfare. But since Solomon Islands was a British possession, its inhabitants were quickly enlisted in the battle against Japanese occupation.

In Chapter 1, I discussed the various ways islanders contributed to the Allied war effort in the Solomon Islands Campaign. I have shown the foundation the Royal Australian Navy built in the protectorate through the construction of the coastwatching network prior to the war, and the significance of this establishment during the Japanese and Allied occupation of the islands. Under the authority of the navy's network, islanders were enlisted as coastwatchers, scouts and labourers. Islanders were mobilised to perform various tasks, including gathering intelligence on Japanese troops, undertaking search and rescue missions, conducting guerrilla war against Japanese forces, facilitating a communication network between Allied troops and coastwatchers, and providing logistical support for both coastwatchers and the Allied armies. A relatively small number of Solomon Islanders were enlisted in the British Solomon Islands Defence Force, becoming members of Allied military units and participating in frontline combat throughout the Solomons and as far as Bougainville. A more significant number of islanders were recruited into the Native

Labour Corps, forming the backbone of the Allied logistical effort and enduring hardships of war arguably on a par with any military fighting force involved.

In Chapter 2, I explored the reasons why Solomon Islanders were generally 'loyal' to the Allies. Islanders did not simply support the Allies because of any anticipated benefit from their contribution. I argue that 'loyalty' was an Allied concept and a postwar simplification. The reasons that lured or motivated islander participation in the war alongside Allied troops were varied in nature, reflecting the complexities of the politics of colonialism and war. Some of these issues of motivation were inscribed in the cultural system itself. Issues of social obligation to the crown were influenced by existing cultural hierarchies, as well as religious practices, especially Christianity. The structure of the big man prestige system and the allegiance demanded by big men and chiefs fostered an indigenous culture of compliance to local authorities without any active forum for criticising their legitimacy. This structure was supported by the principles of Christianity as taught by missionaries and understood by islanders, and was co-opted by the colonial authorities for administration of indigenous affairs.

The effectiveness of Allied propaganda played a significant role in shaping the perceptions of islanders towards Japanese soldiers. The negative image spread among islanders by district officers and missionaries about Japanese soldiers was very successful in its aim to dissuade islanders from providing any form of assistance to the Japanese. This negative image was reinforced through the behaviour of some Japanese soldiers towards islanders and their property during the course of the war. However, severe penalties were also imposed by coastwatchers and district officers upon indigenous peoples if they chose to assist Japanese soldiers. Corporal punishment and withholding wages were common penalties inflicted on local people who were found to provide any form of military or humanitarian assistance to Japanese soldiers.

Although in some areas indigenous peoples were coerced into favouring the Allies, it is evident that the young male population of the time participated in the war driven mainly by curiosity and a sense of adventure, as well as their interest in witnessing the military prowess and social attitudes of both Japanese and Allied troops. These perceptions were very detailed in nature, enabling islanders to distinguish different Allied troops according to their nationalities, with an attitude of favouritism developing towards American troops. This attitude is essential for understanding the escalation of sociopolitical initiatives in the islands after the war.

The impact the war had on island societies and understandings of the outside world was extensive. As discussed in Chapter 3, the war provided opportunities for interracial relations that had not been possible during the prewar period. The racial line was bridged when islanders saw for the first time that black American soldiers and soldiers from other Pacific island countries were capable of doing the same tasks as white soldiers. The opportunity for indigenous peoples to perform jobs of the same nature as their white colonial 'masters' drastically changed local reception of white master/black servant relationships. Furthermore, the easygoing and liberal attitude of white American soldiers towards islanders lay in stark contrast to the prewar British conduct towards indigenous peoples. Islanders were able to share food with white American soldiers, sleep in the same tents and eat from the same plates. Little evidence has come to light of racism by white American soldiers towards islanders, and this easygoing relationship with white GIs altered islander attitudes and expectations of the colonial administration. Witnessing an apparent equality between black and white GIs, at least in uniform, work and diet, also impressed islanders. While these wartime interracial relationships contrasted sharply with levels of racism within the United States at the time, they provided an interactive environment for islanders with white people that had not been possible before the war.

The war shifted the British Solomon Islands Protectorate from a neglected colonial backwater into a new era. Impacts of the war were not limited to interracial encounters. There was also an economic boost in the protectorate. The wage rate increased threefold compared to the prewar period, and the selling of crafts and food to both Japanese and American soldiers increased monetary circulation at the village level. The war also shifted commercial practices between islanders, from the traditional forms of goods exchange using the barter system to the selling of goods and services for cash.

The effects of the war were economically and politically far-reaching. Politically, the protonationalist movement called Maasina Rule gained momentum, raising islander voices for the first time in the protectorate. Although the movement only influenced some sections of the indigenous population, it reflected a degree of grievance held by all islanders, especially a desire for more equality and the representation of islanders in the administration of the protectorate. Hence, Maasina Rule became the voice of islanders in the struggle for increased wages, as well as the demand for the provision of welfare services for indigenous peoples by the administration. Although the movement was unsuccessful, it marked a point in the protectorate's history when islanders gained greater sociopolitical understandings and economic knowledge.

Economically, the military infrastructure left behind became the starting point for economic reconstruction in the protectorate. Roads, bridges, airfields, wharves, permanent buildings and Quonset huts formed a foundation for establishing a modern economy after the war. However, the concentration of this economic restoration initiative on Guadalcanal created long-term problems for social and political development, problems that had they even been foreseen were secondary to the immediate necessity of exploiting development on Guadalcanal. Other islands languished and the population of rural migrants in Honiara began to grow.

Like other islanders in the Pacific, indigenous inhabitants of the British Solomon Islands Protectorate experienced both immediate and long-term impacts of the war. Some of these impacts allowed islanders to benefit from the outside world. Others, although beneficial in the short term for postwar reformation of the economic and political administration of the protectorate, lingered to contribute to the experience of sociopolitical upheaval, culminating 20 years after political independence from Britain in the crisis of 1998–2003. After five years of sociopolitical tension and armed conflict, the nation again found itself in the process of economic, social and political restoration. Although the Regional Assistance Mission to Solomon Islands was successful in restoring law and order in the country, there still remain apprehensive feelings among the people, particularly between those of Guadalcanal and Malaita. Acknowledging this lingering distrust and addressing it in a collective manner would help in restoring a sense of national unity and identity, and it was this realisation that gave birth to the idea of creating a national monument commemorating islanders in the Solomon Islands Campaign.

For an ethnically divided nation, the war was a common denominator and a time in which Solomon Islanders worked together for a common cause. The reminder of this cooperative effort through the physical presence of the Pride of Our Nation monument is symbolically helping to restore that cooperative spirit. In order for this understanding to gain momentum,

6. CONCLUSION

people need to be aware of the history of islander participation in the war. While the monument is testimony to this legacy, the inclusion of islander wartime histories in the national curriculum is intended to encourage younger generations to appreciate the efforts of their ancestors and perhaps begin to develop a sense of pride and national identity.

The Pride of Our Nation monument serves both a political and psychological end in promoting national unity and creating a venue for rebuilding national identity while recognising the contribution of Solomon Islanders during the Pacific Campaign of World War II. With the inclusion of these histories in the school curriculum, it is hoped that more awareness will be raised among the young and future generations of Solomon Islanders, aiding the purpose of instilling a shared sense of national pride and identity.

Appendix 1: Prime Minister Derek Sikua's letter of endorsement of the Solomon Scouts and Coastwatchers Trust

THE PRIME MINISTER

P O BOX G1
HONIARA
SOLOMON ISLANDS

When the organizers of the Coastwatchers & Solomons Scouts Memorial approached me about the possibility of a letter of endorsement from the Government of the Solomon Islands, I immediately and enthusiastically agreed to their request.

Honouring, through the Monument, the bravery, loyalty, and courage of the Solomon Scouts and Coastwatchers will not only do much to ensure that their heroic deeds are immortalised in the minds of Solomon Islanders.

The Monument's statue and Honor Role listing the names of the Coastwatchers and Solomon Scouts will also contribute to fostering in the people of the Solomon Islands a sense of national pride and a shared sense of national identity.

With this in mind, let it be known to all concerned, that the Government of the Solomon Islands wholeheartedly endorses, in the name of the People of the Solomon Islands, the worthy efforts of the Coastwatchers & Solomons Scouts Memorial Trust, and that any forthcoming support from donors to achieving their goal would be greatly appreciated by the Solomon Islands Government and its citizens.

As Prime Minister, I wish to make clear how important I consider this project, and to underscore the Coastwatchers and Solomons Scouts Memorial's historic and present day significance to the People of the Solomon Islands.

I look forward to the day the Memorial is dedicated, for it will be a day of happiness and solemnity, celebration and recognition; a very special day indeed.

Sincerely,

Dr. Derek Silkua
Prime Minister

Source: Solomon Scouts and Coastwatchers Trust.

Appendix 2: Letter of recognition from President Barack Obama

THE WHITE HOUSE
WASHINGTON

July 27, 2012

I am pleased to join in honoring the tremendous contributions Coastwatchers and Solomon Scouts made to the cause of freedom during World War II. Their efforts helped save the Pacific, and they are worthy of the highest praise and recognition.

The landing of United States Marines on Guadalcanal on August 7, 1942, marked the beginning of the arduous journey to victory in the Pacific theater. Were it not for the brave Americans, Solomon Islanders, and other Allied Forces who fought side-by-side during the Battle of Guadalcanal, history might have looked very different.

As we commemorate the 70th anniversary of this crucial campaign, we recall that its success owed much to the critical intelligence provided by the Coastwatchers and the Solomon Scouts. Operating under constant threat and from behind enemy lines, they risked their lives so others would know freedom. They demonstrated the resourcefulness and commitment to duty that became the hallmark of the independant Solomon Islands, and when Solomon Scouts rescued Navy LTGJ John F. Kennedy after his PT boat was sunk, they secured a lasting place in history.

On this special occasion, I commend all those who have worked to ensure the legacy of the Solomon Scouts and Coastwatchers is preserved for future generations. I wish you all the best for the years to come.

APPENDIX 2

Source: Solomon Scouts and Coastwatchers Trust.

Bibliography

Archival sources and interviews

Aruhuri, Paula. 2003. Bruno Nana: A Guadalcanal Scout During World War 2. A Personal Documentation (Jane Kanas-Matebasia, ed.). Port Vila. A copy is in the possession of the author.

Bogese, George. n.d. Prisoner of War/Internee. National Archives of Australia. NAA: MP1103/1, PS19401, Melbourne.

Butoa, Festus. 2015. Oral Recollection. Interviewed by Noela Kaisi, 18 February. Paripao village, Guadalcanal: Solomon Scouts and Coastwatchers Trust.

Crowe, Peter. 1987. Interview with William Bennett, Alfred Alasasa Bisili and Loyd Gina, 3 July. Honiara. A copy of the original audio file is in the possession of the author.

Farland, Merle. Nov 1941 – Feb 1943. Diary and index of Sister Merle Farland. Pacific Manuscripts Bureau, PMB MS 1106. Canberra: The Australian National University.

Innes, John. 2012. Guide to the Guadalcanal Battle Field. Unpublished document. Honiara. A copy of the original is in the possession of the author.

Kennedy, Donald. 1943. District Officer's Report on Coastwatching in the Central and North Western Districts of the British Solomon Islands Protectorate. BSIP 1/III/F5/45. Honiara: Solomon Islands National Archives.

Marchant, William S. 1943a. Letter to Martin Clemens, 22 February. BSIP 5/1, F1/4. Honiara: Solomon Islands National Archives.

Marchant, William S. 1943b. Letter to Western Pacific High Commissioner, 11 March. BSIP 5/1, 13. Honiara: Solomon Islands National Archives.

Meek to High Commissioner, 22 June 1922, WPHC 4, 1862/22, Western Pacific Archives.

Ngwae'hera, Bethlyn. 2015. Oral Recollection. Interviewed by Annie Kwai, 20 December. Honiara: Solomon Scouts and Coastwatchers Trust.

Saunders, Bruce. 2013. Royal Australian Navy Monument Unveiling Speech, 7 August. Honiara: Solomon Scouts and Coastwatchers Trust.

Solomon Islands National Archives. 1945. Labour Corps, BSIP 1/III/9/45, PT.I. Honiara: Solomon Islands National Archives.

Solomon Scouts and Coastwatchers Memorial Trust. 2010. Press conference, 5 March. Honiara.

Tadangoana, Oneisimo. 2011. Oral Recollection. Recorded by Adrian Richardson and Annie Kwai, 25 July. Honiara: Solomon Scouts and Coastwatchers Trust.

WPA (Western Province Assembly). 1988. Western Province and the Second World War. Unpublished oral histories, recorded by Robert King, J.H. Tonga and Patrick Purcell. Original recordings are held at the National Archives of Solomon Islands and Solomon Islands National Museum.

Films

Innes, John. 2012. *Guadalcanal Battlefield Tour*. Trad Records, Honiara: Solomon Scouts and Coastwatchers Trust.

Pike, Andrew, Hank Nelson, Gavan Daws, John Waiko and The Australian National University. 1982. *Angels of War*. Canberra: Research School of Pacific Studies.

Published sources

ABC Radio Australia. 2012. Solomon Islands to Take American Name off Airport to Recognise Japan, 30 March. www.radioaustralia.net.au/pacific/2003-05-19/solomon-islands-to-take-american-name-off-airport-to-recognise-japan/701114.

Akin, David. 2013. *Colonialism, Maasina Rule, and the Origins of Malaitan Kastom*. Honolulu: University of Hawai'i Press. doi.org/10.21313/hawaii/9780824838140.001.0001

Allen, Michael. 1984. Elders, Chiefs, and Big Men: Authority Legitimation and Political Evolution in Melanesia. *American Ethnologist* 11(1): 20–41. doi.org/10.1525/ae.1984.11.1.02a00020

Altobello, Brian. 2000. *Into the Shadows Furious: The Brutal Battle for New Georgia*. Novato, CA: Presidio Press.

Aquilani, H. 2011. Pride of Our Nation Monument. View Point: Letters to the Editor, *Solomon Star*, 8 August: 6.

Armbruster, Stefan. 2013. Australia Finally Recognises Solomons WW2 Vets. SBS Australia Podcast, 25 July. www.sbs.com.au/news/article/2013/07/25/australia-finally-recognises-solomons-ww2-vets.

Ashplant, T.G., Graham Dawson and Michael Roper (eds). 2000. *The Politics of War Memory and Commemoration*. London: Routledge.

Bates, Roma. 1999. The Unveiling of the Coastwatchers Memorial Lighthouse at Madang on 15 August 1959. *Una Voce*. Papua New Guinea Association of Australia. pngaa.net/Library/CoastwatcherMemorial.html.

Belshaw, Cyril S. 1950. *Island Administration in the South West Pacific: Government and Reconstruction in New Caledonia, the New Hebrides and the British Solomon Islands*. London: Royal Institute of International Affairs.

Bennett, Judith. 2002. Roots of Conflict in Solomon Islands. Though Much Is Taken, Much Abides: Legacies of Tradition and Colonialism. *SSGM Discussion Paper* 5. Canberra: State, Society and Governance in Melanesia, The Australian National University.

Bennett, Judith A. 2009. *Natives and Exotics: World War II and Environment in the Southern Pacific*. Honolulu: University of Hawai'i Press. doi.org/10.21313/hawaii/9780824832650.001.0001

Bennett, William. 1988. Behind Japanese Lines in the Western Solomons. In G.M. White, D.W. Gegeo, D. Akin and K. Watson-Gegeo (eds), *The Big Death: Solomon Islanders Remember World War II [Bikfala Faet: Olketa Solomon Aelanda Rimembarem Wol Wo Tu]*. Solomon Islands College of Higher Education and the University of the South Pacific. Suva: Institute of Pacific Studies, 133–148.

Bisili, Alfred A. 1988. Scouting in the Western Solomons. In H. Laracy and G. White (eds), *Taem Blong Faet: World War II in Melanesia. O'O: A Journal of Solomon Islands Studies*. Special Issue 4. Honiara: Solomon Islands Centre, 79–83.

Butcher, Mike. 2012. *'… When the Long Trick's Over': Donald Kennedy in the Pacific*. Bendigo: Holland House Publishing.

Clemens, Martin W. 1998. *Alone on Guadalcanal: A Coastwatcher's Story*. Annapolis, MD: Naval Institute Press.

COI (Central Office of Information). 1946. *Among Those Present*. London: His Majesty's Stationary Office.

Cooper, Harold. 1945. A Dutchman's One-Man War on Guadalcanal. *Pacific Islands Monthly*, 24 August: 8–9.

Daudau, Atrick, Edwin Ha'ahoroa, John Aonima and Julian Treadaway (eds). 2013. *Solomon Islands Social Studies Year 8 Learner's Book*. Melbourne: Pearson.

Falgout, Suzanne. 1991. Lessons of War from Pohnpei. In G.M. White (ed.), *Remembering the Pacific War*. Occasional Paper 36. Honolulu: Center for Pacific Islands Studies, University of Hawai'i at Mānoa, 123–131.

Feldt, Eric. 1991. *The Coastwatchers*. Melbourne: Penguin Books. (Originally published 1946, Oxford University Press.)

Feuer, A.B. (ed.) 1992. *Coastwatching in WWII: Operations against the Japanese on the Solomon Islands, 1941–43*. Westport, CT: Greenwood Publishing.

Fifi'i, Jonathan. 1988. World War II and the Origins of Maasina Rule: One Kwaio View. In G.M. White, D.W. Gegeo, D. Akin and K. Watson-Gegeo (eds), *The Big Death: Solomon Islanders Remember World War II [Bikfala Faet: Olketa Solomon Aelanda Rimembarem Wol Wo Tu]*. Solomon Islands College of Higher Education and the University of the South Pacific. Suva: Institute of Pacific Studies, 216–226.

Fifi'i, Jonathan. 1989. *From Pig-Theft to Parliament: My Life between Two Worlds* (R.M. Keesing, ed.). Suva: Institute of Pacific Studies.

Fifi'i, Jonathan. 1991. Remembering the War in the Solomons. In G.M. White (ed.), *Remembering the Pacific War*. Occasional Paper 36. Honolulu, Hawai'i: Center for Pacific Islands Studies, School of Hawaiian, Asian, and Pacific Studies, University of Hawai'i at Mānoa, 37–46.

Gasa, Biuku and Eroni Kumana. 1988. Oral Accounts from Solomon Islanders. PT-109: The Scouts' Story. In H. Laracy and G. White (eds), *Taem Blong Faet: World War II in Melanesia. O'O: A Journal of Solomon Islands Studies*. Special Issue 4. Honiara: Solomon Islands Centre, 85–95.

Gegeo, David W. 1988. The Big Death: What Pacific Islanders Can Teach Us about World War II. In H. Laracy and G.M. White (eds), *Taem Blong Faet: World War II in Melanesia. O'O: A Journal of Solomon Islands Studies*. Special Issue 4. Honiara: Solomon Islands Centre, 7–13.

Gegeo, David W. 1991. World War II in the Solomons: Its Impact on Society, Politics, and World View. In G.M. White (ed.), *Remembering the Pacific War*. Occasional Paper 36. Honolulu: Center for Pacific Islands Studies, University of Hawai'i at Mānoa, 27–35.

Green, R.C. 1976. The History of Post-Spanish European Contact in the Eastern District before 1939. In R.C. Green and M.M. Creswell (eds), *Southeast Solomon Islands Cultural History: A Preliminary Survey*. Wellington: The Royal Society of New Zealand Bulletin, 31–46.

Hereniko, V. 1999. Representation of Cultural Identities. In V. Hereniko and R. Wilson (eds), *Inside Out: Literature, Cultural Politics, and Identity in the New Pacific*. Lanham: Rowman & Littlefield, 137–166.

Hilliard, D. 1978. *God's Gentlemen: A History of the Melanesian Mission, 1849–1942*. St Lucia: University of Queensland Press.

Horton, Dick C. 1970. *Fire Over the Islands: The Coast Watchers of the Solomons*. Sydney: Reed.

Jersey, Stanley C. 2008. *Hell's Islands: The Untold Story of Guadalcanal*. Texas: A&M University Press.

Kabutaulaka, Tarcisius Tara. 1990. A Socio-political Pressure Group: A Study of the Moro Movement of Guadalcanal. *O'O: A Journal of Solomon Islands Studies* 2(2): 42–62.

Kari, John and Andrew Langabaea. 1988. Oral Accounts from Solomon Islanders. In H. Laracy and G. White (eds), *Taem Blong Faet: World War II in Melanesia. O'O: A Journal of Solomon Islands Studies*. Special Issue 4. Honiara: Solomon Islands Centre, 95–105.

Keesing, Roger M. 1978. Politico-Religious Movements and Anticolonialism on Malaita: Maasina Rule in Historical Perspective. *Oceania* 48(4): 241–261. doi.org/10.1002/j.1834-4461.1978.tb01350.x

Kenilorea, Peter. 2011. Pride of Our Nation Memorial Monument Launch. *Solomon Star*, 8 August: 5.

Kennedy, D. 1946. This Is the Solomon Islander. In R.W. Robson and J. Tudor (eds), *Where the Trade-Wind Blows: Stories and Sketches of the South Pacific Islands*. Sydney: Pacific Publications.

King, Alex. 1999. Memorials of the Great War. In A. Forty and S. Küchler (eds), *The Art of Forgetting*. Oxford: Berg Publishers, 147–165.

Koburger, Charles W., Jr. 1995. *Pacific Turning Point: The Solomons Campaign, 1942–1943*. Westport, CT: Praeger.

Küchler, Susanne. 1999. The Place of Memory. In A. Forty and S. Küchler (eds), *The Art of Forgetting*. Oxford: Berg Publishers.

Laracy, Hugh (ed.). 1983. *Pacific Protest: The Maasina Rule Movement, Solomon Islands, 1944–1952*. Suva: Institute of Pacific Studies, University of the South Pacific.

Laracy, Hugh. 1988. Missionaries and the European Evacuation of the Solomons, 1942–1943. In H. Laracy and G.M. White (eds), *Taem Blong Faet: World War II in Melanesia. O'O: A Journal of Solomon Islands Studies*. Special Issue 4. Honiara: Solomon Islands Centre, 27–34.

Laracy, Hugh. 1991. George Bogese: "Just a Bloody Traitor"? In G.M. White (ed.), *Remembering the Pacific War*. Occasional Paper 36. Honolulu: Center for Pacific Islands Studies, University of Hawai'i at Mānoa, 59–75.

Laracy, Hugh. 2013. *Watriama and Co: Further Pacific Islands Portraits*. Canberra: ANU E Press. doi.org/10.26530/OAPEN_459999

Laracy, Hugh and Geoffrey White (eds). 1988. *Taem Blong Faet: World War II in Melanesia. O'O: A Journal of Solomon Islands Studies.* Special Issue 4. Honiara: Solomon Islands Centre.

Larsen, Colin R. 1946. *Pacific Commandos: New Zealanders and Fijians in Action. A History of Southern Independent Commando and First Commando Fiji Guerrillas*. Wellington, NZ: Reed Publishing.

Leckie, Robert. 2010. *Helmet for My Pillow: From Parris Island to the Pacific*. New York: Bantam Books.

Lindsay, Patrick. 2010. *The Coast Watchers: The Men Behind Enemy Lines Who Saved the Pacific*. Sydney: William Heinemann.

Lindstrom, L. 1984. Doctor, Lawyer, Wise Man, Priest: Big-Men and Knowledge in Melanesia. *Man* 19(2): 291–309. doi.org/10.2307/2802282

Lord, Walter. 1977. *Lonely Vigil: Coastwatchers of the Solomons*. London: Penguin Books.

Luxton, C.T.J. 1955. *Isles of Solomon: A Tale of Missionary Adventure*. Auckland: Methodist Foreign Missionary Society of New Zealand.

MacQuarrie, Hector. 1945. *Vouza and the Solomon Islands*. London: Victor Gollancz.

Maelalo, George. 1988. In the Thick of the Fighting. In G.M. White, D.W. Gegeo, D. Akin and K. Watson-Gegeo (eds), *The Big Death: Solomon Islanders Remember World War II [Bikfala Faet: Olketa Solomon Aelanda Rimembarem Wol Wo Tu]*. Solomon Islands College of Higher Education and the University of the South Pacific. Suva: Institute of Pacific Studies, 175–196.

Matisoo-Smith, E., R.M. Roberts, G.J. Irwin, J.S. Allen, D. Penny and D.M. Lambert. 1998. Patterns of Prehistoric Human Mobility in Polynesia Indicated by mtDNA from the Pacific Rat. *PNAS: Proceedings of the National Academy of Sciences of the United States of America* 95(25): 15145–15150. doi.org/10.1073/pnas.95.25.15145

McQuarrie, Peter. 1994. *Strategic Atolls: Tuvalu and the Second World War.* Christchurch: Macmillan Brown Centre for Pacific Studies, University of Canterbury.

Merillat, Herbert C.L. 2010. *The Island: A History of the First Marine Division on Guadalcanal, August 7 – December 9, 1942.* Yardley, PA: Westholme Publishing.

Michener, James. 1951. *Return to Paradise.* New York: Random House.

Miller, John. 1995. *Guadalcanal: The First Offensive.* Washington, DC: Centre for Military History, United States Army.

Naitoro, John. 2000. *Solomon Islands Conflict: Demands for Historical Rectification and Restorative Justice.* Pacific Updates on Solomon Islands, Fiji and Vanuatu. Canberra: National Centre for Development Studies, The Australian National University.

Nelson, Hank. 1978. From Kanaka to Fuzzy Wuzzy Angel. *Labour History* (35): 172–188. doi.org/10.2307/27508343

Nelson, Hank. 2006. The Enemy at the Door: Australia and New Guinea in World War II. In Y. Toyoda and H. Nelson (eds), *The Pacific War in Papua New Guinea: Memories and Realities.* Tokyo: Centre for Asian Area Studies, Rikkyo University.

Ngwadili, Arnon and Isaac Gafu. 1988. Malaita Refuge, Guadalcanal Labour Corps. In G.M. White, D.W. Gegeo, D. Akin and K. Watson-Gegeo (eds), *The Big Death: Solomon Islanders Remember World War II [Bikfala Faet: Olketa Solomon Aelanda Rimembarem Wol Wo Tu].* Solomon Islands College of Higher Education and the University of the South Pacific. Suva: Institute of Pacific Studies, 197–215.

NPSI (National Parliament of Solomon Islands). 2013. CPA UK Delegation Honours Coast Watchers Monument, 25 February. Honiara.

Osifelo, Frederick. 1985. *Kanaka Boy: An Autobiography*. Suva: Institute of Pacific Studies.

Pacific Islands Forum Secretariat. n.d. *The Forum Principles of Good Leadership and Accountability. Country Report — Solomon Islands*, 171–195. www.forumsec.org/pages.cfm/political-governance-security/good-governance/forum-principles-of-good-leadership-accountability.html.

Pacific Islands Monthly. 1973. Only Ghosts on San Jorge … But Search for Japanese Soldiers Unearths 'Skeletons' in the Closet. *Pacific Islands Monthly*, July: 5–6.

Pospisil, Leopold J. 1958. *Kapauku Papuans and Their Law*. Publications in Anthropology 54. New Haven: Yale University.

Prados, John. 2013. *Islands of Destiny: The Solomons Campaign and the Eclipse of the Rising Sun*. New York: Penguin Group.

Reed, Liz. 1999. 'Part of Our Own Story': Representations of Indigenous Australians and Papua New Guineans within *Australia Remembers 1945–1995* — The Continuing Desire for a Homogeneous National Identity. *Oceania* 69(3): 157–170. doi.org/10.1002/j.1834-4461.1999.tb02710.x

Riseman, Noah. 2010. Australian [Mis]Treatment of Indigenous Labour in World War II Papua and New Guinea. *Labour History* 98: 163–182. doi.org/10.5263/labourhistory.98.1.163

Rogerson, Emma. 2012. *The 'Fuzzy Wuzzy Angels': Looking Beyond the Myth*. SVSS Paper. Canberra: Australian War Memorial.

Rowland, Michael. 1999. Remembering to Forget. In A. Forty and S. Küchler (eds), *The Art of Forgetting*. Oxford: Berg Publishers.

Ryan, Peter. 1969. The Australia and New Guinea Administrative Unit (ANGAU). In *The History of Melanesia*. Second Waigani Seminar. Canberra: Research School of Pacific Studies, The Australian National University, 531–548.

Sahlins, Marshall D. 1963. Poor Man, Rich Man, Big-Man, Chief: Political Types in Melanesia and Polynesia. *Comparative Studies in Society and History* 5(3): 285–303. doi.org/10.1017/S0010417500001729

Saunders, Keithie. 2013. *Of Wars and Worship: The Extraordinary Story of Gertrude and Alvin Blum*. Oxford: George Ronald.

Silata, Walingai P.B. 1988. Oral Accounts of Second World War Experiences of the People of the Huon Peninsula, Morobe Province, Papua New Guinea. In H. Laracy and G. White (eds), *Taem Blong Faet: World War II in Melanesia. O'O: A Journal of Solomon Islands Studies*. Special Issue 4. Honiara: Solomon Islands Centre, 63–74.

Solomon Star. 2013. Local Scouts and Coastwatchers Recognized, 11 August.

Solomon Times Online. 2008. Memorial Service Held for Japanese Soldiers of WW2, 16 September. www.solomontimes.com/news/memorial-service-held-for-japanese-soldiers-of-ww2/2590.

Tregaskis, Richard. 1943. *Guadalcanal Diary*. New York: Random House.

Waiko, John. 1991. Oral History and the War: The View from Papua New Guinea. In G.M. White (ed.), *Remembering the Pacific War*. Occasional Paper 36. Honolulu: Center for Pacific Islands Studies, University of Hawai'i at Mānoa, 3–16.

Wheatley family. 2015. In Memory of Dr Hugh Wheatley. Born 13 Oct 1913. Died May 1944. *Solomon Star*, 13 October: 8.

White, Geoffrey M. 1995. Remembering Guadalcanal: National Identity and Transnational Memory-Making. *Public Culture* 7(3): 529–555. doi.org/10.1215/08992363-7-3-529

White, Geoffrey M. 2015. The Coastwatcher Mythos: The Politics and Poetics of Solomon Islands War Memory. In G. Carr and K. Reeves (eds), *Heritage and Memory of War: Responses from Small Islands*. New York: Routledge, 194–216.

White, Geoffrey M., David W. Gegeo, David Akin and Karen Watson-Gegeo (eds). 1988. *The Big Death: Solomon Islanders Remember World War II [Bikfala Faet: Olketa Solomon Aelanda Rimembarem Wol Wo Tu]*. Solomon Islands College of Higher Education and the University of the South Pacific. Suva: Institute of Pacific Studies.

Wurm, Stephen A. and Shirô Hattori (eds). 1981–83. *Language Atlas of the Pacific Area*. Pacific Linguistics Series C 66–67. Canberra: Australian Academy of the Humanities in collaboration with the Japan Academy.

Zaku, Steven V., Leslie Miki, James Sao and Henry Vasula. 1988. Scouting and Fighting in Santa Isabel. In G.M. White, D.W. Gegeo, D. Akin and K. Watson-Gegeo (eds), *The Big Death: Solomon Islanders Remember World War II [Bikfala Faet: Olketa Solomon Aelanda Rimembarem Wol Wo Tu]*. Solomon Islands College of Higher Education and the University of the South Pacific. Suva: Institute of Pacific Studies, 149–174.

www.ingramcontent.com/pod-product-compliance
Lightning Source LLC
Chambersburg PA
CBHW061255230426
43662CB00028B/2454